Humour in Memoriam

Humour in Memoriam

George Mikes

London   Routledge & Kegan Paul

in association with André Deutsch

First published 1970
by Routledge and Kegan Paul Ltd
Broadway House, 68–74 Carter Lane
London EC4
Printed in Great Britain
by Western Printing Services Ltd, Bristol
© George Mikes 1970

SBN 7100 6687 2

Contents

Acknowledgments

The author would like to thank Simon & Schuster Inc. for permission to reprint the diagram from Max Eastman, *The Enjoyment of Laughter*, copyright © 1931 by H. T. Webster, p. 351; and A. D. Peters & Company and the Macmillan Company, New York for permission to reprint three diagrams from Arthur Koestler, *The Act of Creation*, 1964, pp. 35, 37 and 41.

In Remembrance

'Comedy is a way of making money; the trouble is that everyone nowadays tries to make it into a philosophical system.' It was not Sigmund Freud who said this but a much more 'with-it' sage of our era, Mr Spike Milligan. I have a tremendous respect for both Freud and Mr Milligan, but surely the latter was wrong on this particular occasion. He ought to have said: 'Humour is philosophy; the trouble is that everyone nowadays tries to make money out of it.'

How wrong can you get? Certainly considerably more wrong than Mr Milligan. A leading article in the *Twentieth Century* (in a special number devoted to comedy) declared: 'Surely, there has never been an epoch in human history when professional laughter-makers . . . enjoyed so much power, wealth and kudos as in the age of the H bomb.' Professional laughter-makers. *yes*; humorous writers: *no*. Professional laughter-makers include the funny men on television, their scriptwriters, their gag-men, female impersonators, cockney prophets and the slightly more sophisticated clowns posing as sages, the whole sorry lot in hot (and, as a rule, successful) pursuit of cash. The group of humorous writers, sadly left behind in the race, includes not only the so-called professional humorists but almost any writer with a strong humorous vein who is able and willing to rise above the level of smear and cheap sarcasm.

The truth is that humour, as we have known it, is dying.

By a curious coincidence, it was only yesterday – the day before starting on this book – that I had lunch with an old friend and colleague, Ephraim Kishon, the national humorist of Israel. The lunch was a gloomy affair. (Many people – see Popular Fallacy No. 4 – believe that a lunch between two humorists could not possibly have been anything else.) We both mourned humour which, obviously, lay on its death-bed. It was no good deluding ourselves just because we loved the patient, indeed the *moriturus*. Humour was on its deathbed and we realized with sadness that we were among the last Mohicans of a species called – usually derisively – humorists. I was sadder than Kishon. Not because I loved the patient more; not at all: he loved him just as much; but because I was slower in noticing the sad phenomenon and was too late in deserting the sinking ship: humorous writing. Kishon started writing comedies, then films, and went on to direct and produce films. Humour may die but Kishon will laugh.

I personally went on writing my funny books. They became funnier and funnier, and a gallant and noble breed of men went on reading them out of force of habit. But it was no good; humorous writing is a dying trade like those of the baker, and the candlestick-maker; or a dying art like that of the goldsmith. I was a circus-artist, performing on a dying horse. What's the use of the rider improving his skill and artistry when the horse under him is about to expire? When the horse is tottering and his knees are about to give in?

Two great experts on and practitioners of humour – William Davis, the new editor of *Punch*, and William Shawn, the old editor of the *New Yorker* – know better. 'There is a humour-crisis,' concluded Mr Davis, summing up a chat with Mr Shawn (*Punch*, February 5, 1969). He quotes Mr Shawn as saying that he had diagnosed, at least in the United States, a positive reaction against humour.

'The younger generation especially,' said Mr Shawn, 'has no time for [humour]. The word "funny" doesn't exist for them, except as a form of abuse. They react to cruelty – and to a situation of hopelessness and despair – as if it were humour.'

The editor of the *New Yorker* also remarked that gaiety had completely gone out of humour. He added:

'Everything has become mechanical and cruel. The idea that some-thing might be seriously funny seems to be alien to young people today.'

Mr Shawn gave an explanation for this phenomenon which is, how-ever, only part of the story. He said that a lot of talented people who would have given their lives to writing thirty years ago, today took well-paid jobs as TV gagmen, performers and such-like. He ended up with a truly melancholy picture of these people – worthy of a better fate but avoiding it with care – sitting with ten others churning out gags for fifth-rate – well, what if first-rate? – television shows:

'Their talent never has a chance to develop because no one compels them to do a sustained piece of writing and thinking. They don't leave because gag-writing is well paid, and after ten years they are totally unable to write humorous articles.'

This ensuing inability makes them happy. It means that the danger of foolish temptation has passed; they will not – because they will not be able to – give up an hour or two of their profitable time to turn to simple, old-fashioned humorous writing. The humorous book of these days is David Frost's opus: it looks like a book but it isn't.

The basic responsibility lies with society itself. If society appreciated a good writer more than a good gagman, people would stick to writing. Our era, however, is a new era, in the sense that the era of steam and electricity, the era of fast industrialization, were new eras. A new era is an era unsure of itself; and uncertainty has created pomposity and hypocrisy, just as in the Victorian era. Our age cannot afford to laugh at itself because it *is* ridiculous. Ours, of course, is not just a new Victorian era: history, or sociology, does not move in circles but in spirals (and occasionally like a boomerang). Our uncertainty expresses itself in impatience and cruelty and while cruelty is an ingredient of humour, the cruelty of our epoch finds non-humorous outlets for itself. Our age looks at the adventurer with admiration. Its hero is that ass, Superman, who achieves the impossible, and not the chaplinesque bum who fails to accomplish the easiest tasks. We visualize ourselves as mock-heroes yet feel a secret desire to escape from it all. So our boring sham-heroes chase spies, reach for the moon and succeed in living in the future, which is one way of avoiding earthly present.

Humour, as we shall see, has many ingredients, some of them not very attractive. But two of the essential (and attractive) ingredients are wisdom and self-mockery. This age is not wise; and it cannot afford self-mockery.

This is the age of tinned food; it has also become the age of tinned humour, of canned entertainment. Nobody wants the real thing – few indeed remember the original taste of fresh vegetables and unfrozen meat – but as people need *something* – whether it is food or humour – they open tins and take gags, belly-laughs and television comedians for humour.

Sex is still in as another god but sex is slowly dying, too. Mr Cecil King has remarked in an article that Victorians regarded sex as taboo but loved discussing death; today the discussion of sex in all its forms is free, while death has become an obscenity. There are signs and symptoms, however – unrecorded by Mr King – to show that sex is slowly declining and going the way of humour, while death – particularly violent, funny and perverted death – is becoming a new vogue.

This book is an obituary notice on humour. Out of love and respect for the deceased, I shall treat humour as if it were still alive. But humour is dead. It is as dead as Stephen Leacock, Damon Runyon and James Thurber. Some people still read these humorists just as some go and watch the films of Chaplin, Buster Keaton and Harold Lloyd. But where is the film-maker who, in his senses, plans to make a new Buster Keaton, Harold Lloyd or even an old-type Chaplin-film? Humour is as dead as Chaplin, Keaton and Lloyd-films are. It cannot be rescued; it cannot survive. But it can resurrect. This age cannot be the purveyor of humour; but it can – and will, one day – be the proper subject of it.

Part 1   Popular fallacies

Collapsible barbecue

Popular Fallacy No. 1: A Sense of
Humour is the greatest of all gifts
and a man with a Sense of Humour
must be a nice man.

It is natural that surrounding the coffin of Humour, we should pose the
question: what did he die of?

My first thoughts were: he had committed suicide. He looked around
this world, saw what we all see, took an overdose of television, and died.
This theory, however, refutes itself and is untenable. The world is
dreary because Humour is dead; consequently Humour could not have
committed suicide *because* the world was dreary. This would have
meant that Humour committed suicide because he was dead. That
would have been too much of a joke even for Humour.

He had, however, other reasons for suicide. No one understood him.
Indeed, he was almost universally misunderstood. A number of Popular Fallacies crystallized around him and one aim of this work is to
dispel the main fallacies and clear (occasionally perhaps besmirch) the
memory of our Loved One.

There are two further thoughts which keep recurring to me and which,
I feel, I must mention before I get down to my main subject.

First: What is this world going to be like without him?

Contemplating this subject, I kept thinking of my undeservedly rich
friend, Brandeis, from Sydney. When I visited Australia, a new
device, called the Collapsible Barbecue, was all the rage in the land. It
was a barbecue, as its name suggests; but it was not collapsible, as its
name also suggests. (It was portable – but it was certainly not collapsible.) Once upon a time I had a collapsible armchair which, however,
had not been sold to me as such. Brandeis tried to persuade all and
sundry, friend and foe, to buy a collapsible barbecue. For him it was

the invention of the century. One irate visitor asked him why he was so enthusiastic about collapsible barbecues.

'But it has changed our lives,' exclaimed Brandeis.

'How?' the visitor went on enquiring.

Brandeis paused to think, then he replied:

'Well, we used to eat inside and sit outside; now we eat outside and sit inside.'

Plus ça change . . . as someone else put it in other words. I thought the death of Humour would cause about as much change in our lives as the collapsible barbecue caused in Brandeis's, in other words that it would pass practically unnoticed in a world which does not really *need* humour. But this cannot be. After all, it does make a difference in the intellectual climate of the world whether James Thurber or Harry Worth is the representative of its lighter moods; whether its favourite reading is Evelyn Waugh or the comic strip.

My second thought is this. I keep asking myself: What is poor Humour doing now? Is he in Heaven? I am not convinced that there is such a place but if there is, Humour must be bored stiff by all those angels playing Bach on their harps. Hell must be much more amusing and pleasant than Heaven and indeed – as we shall see – he is much likelier to find himself there. He was not such a nice chap as most people tend to believe. Yet . . . our beloved Humour in Hell? . . . a distressing thought.

So I am prepared to agree with the vicar's widow who, when asked about her recently deceased husband, replied irritably:

'Well, I am sure my late husband is enjoying eternal bliss. But must we talk about such an unpleasant subject?'

My father was the wittiest man in Siklos. This, I admit, does not make him the equal of Voltaire, Talleyrand, Oscar Wilde or Dr Johnson. Siklos is just a village in southern Hungary and even when I add that it is now called a 'greater commune' and is a 'district town', somehow I feel that I still fail to impress. Nevertheless, Siklos used to be a boisterous and buoyant place, with a prosperous and well-educated middle class, well-informed of the literary goings-on in Budapest, Vienna and Paris (London was too remote in those days), keenly interested in politics (mostly local – my father was the editor of the town's only newspaper), and with a lively, if necessarily rather provincial cultural life. Siklos had 3,000 inhabitants and my father was the wittiest of these 3,000; I think I can safely throw in all the neighbouring villages, which would make it 5,000.

My father was a lawyer and I was ten years old when he died at the age of forty-two. I remember a lot of people sitting around on occasions in our drawing-room, my father keeping them in stitches of laughter for hours on end. He wrote many songs and sketches for local entertainment and once an operetta of his was a great hit in the neighbouring large town of Pécs. People have quoted to me many of his remarks which they had remembered throughout a lifetime and I, too, remember a few witty and grotesquely original things he said to me.

My mother had a cousin who spoke a great deal of my father here in London, many years after his death. He idolized my father whom he remembered much better than I. He often told me – not critically, indeed admiringly:

'Your father could pull people's legs superbly. He would single out a man – someone pompous or conceited but often simply someone who was silly, slow on the uptake or easily embarrassed – and make him his target. If he proved really vulnerable, your father went for him in the grand manner and massacred him while everybody else roared with laughter at his expense.'

I, too, vaguely remembered these spiritual blood-baths my father was so fond of. And when I heard these stories a half-forgotten memory from my own childhood came creeping back into my mind.

I loved my father; he was – and still is – my hero. In his footsteps I tried to follow to the best of my ability. I am, alas, not the wittiest man of the town *I* live in, but I used to be just as cruel and merciless to my friends as he in his prime. I loved the waves of laughter which accompanied my sallies and onslaughts on outraged and defenceless victims; I enjoyed the admiring glances of pretty girls, the fearful deference of those who might become my victims, and the flashes of red-hot anger in the eyes of humiliated opponents.

One day – I was sixteen or seventeen – a school-friend of mine – Tibor was his Christian name – came to see me and took me to task. He was one of my closest friends, an extremely able young man, a brilliant poet and a born rebel. We were all convinced that he would turn out one of the great poets of his generation. That day, Tibor delivered a severe homily to me about my uncivilized ways. He paid my early literary efforts some compliments but added that I was misusing my gifts: I was too often cruel to people; I was a bully who attacked the weak but avoided the strong. He said that one's spiritual powers were given one to protect the weak against the unjust tyrant; he thought that making a fool of harmless and defenceless people was a worse crime than stealing.

This homily had an immediate and permanent effect on me. After this well-deserved lecture I never again made a weak and helpless person ridiculous; never deliberately humiliated anyone who was not able to defend himself. I tried – I often failed, I know, but at least I tried – to follow Anatole France's advice, not to mock at love and beauty. I am still grateful to Tibor. He is today a successful and respected physician in Budapest. As far as I know he never published a line of poetry in his life and I have not seen him for over thirty years.

I have learned by now that I should, in fact, be most ungrateful and feel hostile to Tibor. His nobility of soul is the cause of my pending downfall; it is more or less general acceptance of his mentality that has killed Humour.

Today I know that Humour is essentially cruel and aggressive; humour is, basically, one specific – perhaps refined, sublimated, disguised – form of cruelty and aggression. This age of ours dotes on cruelty, aggression and self-assertion – and not altogether wrongly as aggression at least, if not cruelty, has its healthy elements. Humour, by denying its very essence, has committed suicide. Yes – it *was* suicide, after all.

In many great practitioners – from Swift through W. S. Gilbert to Evelyn Waugh – a strong streak of cruelty is noticeable and, for weaker souls like myself, disturbing. Others, like Mark Twain, Max Beerbohm or Ogden Nash, seemingly lack it. To deprive humour of its streak of cruelty is like depriving the elephant of its trunk, like depriving water of its wetness. It is like putting a meek, old cow, kindly disposed to the world and to all toreros, in the bull-ring. This sometimes actually happens. The ensuing spectacle is pleasanter, less bloody and less hair-raising than those provided by more spirited animals, but it is not a bullfight. And it does not quite satisfy the crowd which has after all come to watch an unpleasant, bloody and hair-raising spectacle.

The beholder's eye

A humorist is no more an expert on humour than a man suffering from diabetes is an 'expert' on diabetes. He – like the diabetic – has got it, but he has no idea how he got it and still less how to get rid of it.

Humour is a problem of philosophy, but philosophers do not fare much better than humanists or diabetics. A philosopher with a sense of humour will laugh at a joke instead of performing a post mortem on it; and a philosopher will not be able – however competent he may be otherwise – to teach us a lot about the sense of humour if he himself lacks one.

The issue is further plagued by another complication – unique to this subject. A man reading an essay on humour has no more right or reason to expect to laugh or to be entertained than someone reading an essay on Nichomachean Ethics; yet, he does expect to be vastly amused. A woman reading a cookery book does not expect to have her hunger quenched but a person reading an essay on humour does expect to be amused. And the fact that more dull books have been written on humour than on any other subject seems to make no difference.

And perhaps just as well, because enlightened he will not be. Philosophy is a curious subject, in the best case. Philosophers – if I may repeat myself – may count the most brilliant minds of humanity in their ranks; they may have said what they had to say in an exciting, profound, original, subtle and witty *manner*; but their conclusions have never amounted to much. The philosopher is like a good athlete on the double bar; his movements are beautiful; his skill is breath-taking; his achievement admirable. But when he jumps off, he is where he was before he started, he has achieved nothing, he has progressed nowhere.

7

You wonder what all this jumping and bouncing and standing on his head was in aid of. His performance was as useless as it was spectacular. There is not one single statement – however simple, innocuous and self-evident – on which philosophers agree. No philosopher has said *anything* in the course of the last twenty-five centuries which all his fellows accept. In the last two or three millennia not one single statement made by any one of these experts has passed uncontradicted by other, equally qualified and eminent experts.

Humour, as a subject, has fared even worse than most. It has been neglected on the one hand and over-exposed on the other. When – in the fifties – I wrote a book on a number of humorous writers and artists, I found that none of my eight humorists – with the exception of Evelyn Waugh – had been the subject of any serious appreciation; I discovered that in Mr Edmund Wilson's two volumes – being the literary chronicles of the twenties and thirties – James Thurber's name was not even mentioned, and there was only one passing reference to Stephen Leacock; in the Columbia Encyclopaedia there was no entry under 'Humour' or – to be more precise – 'Humor'.

But while individual humorists used to be – and still are – the step-children of literature, humour, as a general subject, has been tackled in an incredibly large number of books, so many, in fact, that their bibliography alone would amount to a considerably heavier volume than this book of mine. I have spent long hours reading and studying quite a few of them and I wish I hadn't. I read, as is usual with philosophy, many brilliant statements and arguments but, in the end, knew no more about humour than at the outset. Most philosophers distinguish between wit, joke and humour – a perfectly legitimate distinction, but they write as if the three belonged to three different, hermetically sealed and strictly non-communicating departments. Having established this principle of segregation, they proceed to mix up the three elements and it is often not clear which one they have in mind. It should also be remembered that humour is an utterly different problem for the philosopher, for the psychologist and for the literary essayist. Having said all this, while I do not intend to give the reader a summary of the innumerable theories, I think I ought to give a sample of them. (I shall return to three of these theories in a little more detail in a subsequent chapter.) I personally do not wish to add yet another theory to the existing ones. Perhaps I might explain here – although I doubt the need for such an explanation – that I am neither a philosopher nor a psychologist; this book is not a scholarly book and does not aim at being one. I am a simple practitioner – a G.P. of humour – I wish to record my thoughts, experiences, problems and the curious, sometimes satisfying, sometimes frustrating relationship between the humorist and his raw material. This is a book of reflections and observations and also the record of a life-long and hopeless love-affair. And now back to my colleagues and predecessors.

The Old Testament already noticed the sadness in laughter: 'Even in laughter the heart is sorrowful; and the end of mirth is heaviness.'
According to Plato, we laugh at the misfortunes of our friends and our feeling is mixed pleasure and pain.[1] Aristotle also recognized the essentially cruel nature of humour and said that to make a joke of a man is to vilify him. Cicero, too, thought that the ridiculous had its grounds in baseness and deformity. A very long jump takes us to John Harrington, who attempts his definition from another angle. Comedies – he says – 'may make men see the shame at their own faults'. Hobbes's definition is the most famous of all – it also takes note of the aggressive element in laughter: 'Laughter,' he says, 'is nothing else but sudden glory arising from a sudden conception of some eminency in ourselves, by comparison with the infirmity of others, or with our own formerly.'
Dr Johnson saw the difficulties and remarked: 'Comedy has been particularly unpropitious in definers . . .' Then he went on to define the notion of comic by itself: 'Every dramatic composition, which raises mirth, is comick.' Had this not been said by Dr Johnson, it would never have been quoted. Lesser men did better. He also knew, however – and few people did – what serious humour meant: 'To raise mirth, it is by no means universally necessary, that the personages should be either mean, or corrupt, nor always requisite, that the action should be trivial, nor ever, that it should be fictitious.' (He also knew that Swift and Pope never laughed, but he himself laughed 'like a rhinoceros'.)
Hegel – true to himself – is very obscure on the subject. Schopenhauer expressed himself with true Teutonic verbosity: 'The cause of laughter in every case is simply sudden perception of the incongruity between a concept and the real object which have been thought through in some relation and the laugh itself is just an expression of this incongruity.'
Paul Carus says: 'We laugh only at petty triumphs.' He added: 'Nothing is in itself ridiculous, but anything will become so as soon as it serves to secure harmless triumph.'

9

Bergson (and more of him and Freud later) noticed 'that laughter was always corrective'. He was also fully aware of the aggressive and cruel nature of laughter: 'In laughter we always find an unavowed intention to humiliate and conseqeuntly to correct our neighbour.'

Lessing also believed in the corrective power of laughter. 'Comedy corrects by laughter, but not by derision.' According to Freud, wit originated from an economy of expenditure in thought, humour from an economy of expenditure in feeling. Freud had a high opinion of humour – not of wit, not of the comic, but of pure humour. He thought humour was one of the highest psychical achievements. 'Humour,' he added, 'is a means of obtaining pressure in spite of the distressing effects that interfere with it.' He also speaks of the 'Grandeur of humour' and – in a later definition – he regards it as an economy of pity. He acknowledges that the frontiers of humour can be expanded to include even horror and disgust.

I could go on for another two hundred pages, just giving brief summaries of views and definitions. The reader may have found quite a few of the remarks quoted interesting and thought-provoking but I doubt if he knows more about humour than before. He may feel himself in the position of that old, blind Jew who asked a young girl what milk was like.

'Milk?' asked the girl, astonished.

'Yes, milk. You see, I am blind and I just can't imagine what milk is like.'

'Well, milk is white.'

'My dear girl,' said the old man, 'I am old and I am blind. I just don't know what *white* means.'

'It's easy to explain,' said the girl helpfully. 'A swan is white.'

'But I have never seen a swan.'

'It has a curved neck.'

'Curved,' sighed the old man. 'It's easy for you to say *curved*. But I don't know what curved is.'

The girl lifted her right arm and bent her wrist forward like a swan's neck.

'Feel it,' she said. 'That's curved.'

The old man felt the girl's arm, touched the curved wrist several times and then exclaimed with satisfaction:

'Thank God! Now at last I know what milk is like.'

A reader, having studied Hegel and two hundred other philosophers of humour, may explain equally joyfully: 'At last, I know what humour is!'

One sympathizes with people – like Max Eastman – who throw their hands up: 'Humour is a human *element*, an instinct, not to be analysed further.' An English translator of Freud, James Strachey, remarked that the English word *humour* seemed to be rarely used by itself, that it hardly occurred except in the phrase *sense of humour*. Then he added, somewhat nonchalantly: 'As for definition the reader will be in a position to decide for himself' – a somewhat pious hope considering that philosophers have been unable to decide for themselves for three thousand years.

For practical purposes, we may agree on two points:

1 We may know a great deal about humour without knowing exactly what humour really is. Physicists can produce electricity; they know all *about* it; with its help they can travel in the air, on land or on the water; they can dig tunnels, remove mountains, transmit messages to the moon or Mars, lighten our darkness and cure the sick with it; yet, they do not know exactly what electricity is.

2 As a working definition, sufficient for our purposes, we might accept the original Latin meaning of the word: humour is a flavour, an essence, simply a way of looking at things.

Humour, like beauty, is in the beholder's eye.

A few years ago, I told Arthur Koestler that I was writing a novel. He asked me what it was about. I told him: about a compulsive eater who ate as many others drank and who, eventually, ate himself to death, with suicidal purpose, on board a French liner. Koestler nodded: 'A good subject. Much better for Kafka than for you; but undoubtedly a good subject.' I laughed. Of course, this would have been a tragic, haunting and nightmarish theme in Kafka's – or in Koestler's – hand: a much better novel, no doubt. I wished I could write Kafka's or Koestler's novels but, alas, I could write only my own. So this had to be a tragi-comic story. Kafka and Koestler would have regarded my hero, Sam Mackay, as a pitiful character and would have sketched him in considerably greater depth than I was able to; I saw the melancholy, indeed tragic, side of him, certainly respected his bear-like dignity, rather liked him on the whole, but I could not help laughing at him. But then I cannot help laughing at Oedipus either.

There are no 'funny' things; there are only things (or sayings or situations) which *you* find funny. Admittedly, there are stories and sayings which more or less educated people all over the world find funny – but not all. Some may not find them funny because they lack what is called a sense of humour; but there may be other reasons for not laughing –

indeed, for actually crying – at a funny story. You may have a side-splitting story about a man whose wife has eloped with a sanitary engineer; but should you tell it to a chap whose wife has, in fact, just eloped with a sanitary engineer, he may pick up a carving knife and stick it in your ribs. He may still, of course, be a man with an excellent sense of humour. Humour, I repeat, is in the beholder's eye and whether two people watching the same event will both find it funny, does not solely depend on their sense of humour but on many other circumstances, including their natural disposition. I, for example, had a very happy childhood and my sister had a rather unhappy childhood but we both had the same childhood; I had loving and devoted parents, my sister had strict and not too devoted parents – but we both had the same parents.

The beauty of aggression

I am now going to point out the nasty elements in humour and try to disprove Popular Fallacy No. 1, namely that a sense of humour is an unreservedly wonderful gift, and that a man with a sense of humour must be a nice man.

While I hope to show that humour can – and usually does – contain a lot of nasty elements, I want to make my own position clear: in spite of this fact, I do believe with Freud, that humour is one of the highest psychical achievements and that it has certain redeeming features which put it among the great gifts of humanity. It is not all snow-white; it is not one hundred per cent beauty and bliss but, warts and all, it deserves our respect and affection.

But, let us begin with the warts.

'Wit is related to aggression, hostility, and sadism; humour is related to depression, narcissism and masochism' – to quote yet another author, Dr Martin Grotjahn, in his book, *Beyond Laughter*.[2] Dr Grotjahn goes over a number of manifestations of humour and we might as well follow in his footsteps. He starts with 'Kidding'. *Kidding* is an American expression but, alas, it needs no explanation in this country either. *Kidding* means to treat someone like a kid, in other words, assume a superior, pseudo-authoritarian attitude towards him. 'The inveterate kidder,' writes Dr Grotjahn, 'expresses his own conflict with authority (usually with his parents) and projects it onto his victim. The kidder imitates his father torturing his "Kid" who is in a position of humiliation and passive endurance. . . . He can dish it out but he cannot take it.'

After the kidder comes the practical joker. He is the eternal adolescent, his aggression is barely disguised. My brother is a mild and compassionate man but with an explosive temperament. He used to be fond of mild practical jokes, but even these were cruel, or at least aggressive enough. For example, if you had a bad cold, my brother was liable to wait for you to feel a sneeze coming on – then he would suddenly jerk your handkerchief away so that you were caught in mid-sneeze and either sneezed into your hand or choked. Not a joke likely to please the most sensitive and susceptible of persons. My brother would also stop someone in the street and ask him if he knew where, say, Bradford Avenue was? The victim would say: No, he didn't know. Then my brother would explain to him – with all due decorum – that it was second on the right.

The second joke is just mildly aggressive; the first has an element of cruelty in it. The third, a well-known one, that follows (not my brother's), aims at humiliating its victim. A man is invited to a nudist party by the practical jokers and he arrives full of expectations. The butler – one of the conspirators – receives him, takes him aside and tells him to undress. When stark naked, he is announced and enters a room where everyone else is properly dressed in evening gowns and dinner jackets – complete with jewels and decorations.

This is, of course, a somewhat awkward situation, and a man appearing stark naked in such circumstances must be prepared for surprised looks and even adverse comment.

The rule is that the victim of this adolescent sadism has to accept the joke good-naturedly, otherwise he is regarded as a bore, with no sense of humour. If he loses his temper, he becomes even more ridiculous and the joke is deemed to have succeeded even better. The only accepted way of retaliation is revenge – i.e. by means of another, even crueller, practical joke. And so on, *da capo sin al fine*.

Take an ordinary remark, generally acknowledged as witty. W. S. Gilbert, many years after Wagner's death, was asked at a party by a lady with high-brow pretensions: 'Tell me, Mr Gilbert, is dear old Richard Wagner still composing?' 'No, Madam,' replied Gilbert, 'actually he is decomposing.'

Or remember one of F. E. Smith's famous rejoinders to the judge who told him off pompously: 'I am afraid, Mr Smith, that even after your opening remarks, I am not much wiser.' 'Not wiser, my Lord,' came the retort, 'but better informed.'

Take the famous quip: 'Psychoanalysis is the disease it pretends to cure'; or take almost any of Wilde's parodies: 'Ah, Meredith! Who can define him? His style is chaos illumined by flashes of lightning. As a writer he has mastered everything except language; as a novelist he can do everything, except tell a story. As an artist he is everything except articulate.'

Or, Wilde again, having been informed that Osgood, the go-ahead publisher who advertised the fact that all his books were published simultaneously in London and New York, had died: 'He is a great loss to us. I suppose they will bury him simultaneously in London and New York.'

If the wit has no other butt, he himself will do. When Wilde was asked to make a few changes in one of his plays, he asked: 'Who am I to tamper with a masterpiece?'

Each of these clever witticisms fills us with the desire: 'I wish I'd said it.' (Even Wilde felt this irresistible desire and once, when applauding one of Whistler's witticisms, he exclaimed: 'I wish I had said that.' Whistler replied, 'You will, Oscar, you will.') But, whatever their charm, all these remarks are offensive, aimed against a victim and designed to establish the wit's superiority over him. Witticism comes easily – even compulsively – to many people. Wit can become a way of life in some circles, literary groups, Central European cafés. It is *bellum omnium contra omnes*, very much with the survival of the fittest. The wit's aim is murder. Everyone is fair game. The witticism is a thinly disguised insult: you are either able to retaliate on the same level or you have to grin as if you enjoyed it. But in these circles – with all the ruthlessness of the game – this blood sport is not altogether unfair. Members of the circle know at least what to expect and in any case, the jokes soon become repetitive, follow a pattern and become an utter bore – yet the players cannot desist; it has indeed become a way of life. The whole thing is altogether cruel (and usually more amusing in its horror) when the hunter finds an innocent and completely unprepared victim, who becomes embarrassed, has no idea how to take it and is inclined to break down in tears.

'The wit . . . is hostile, often with a skilful, artful, highly developed, sophisticated meanness and viciousness,' says Dr Grotjahn, and he compares him to a man who plays with sparks but never lights a warming fire. He thinks that the wit's irresistible tendency to make witty remarks 'is his way of releasing his hostility. Without it, he probably would blow his top or get a migraine attack.'

The cynic is a special type of wit: he is not just a 'distressing faultfinder', as one dictionary defines him. *The Shorter Oxford Dictionary* is much better: The cynic 'is one disposed to decry and sneer at the sincerity or goodness of human motives or actions'. This refusal to believe in human goodness is an essential factor in the cynic – whose name, by the way, comes from an ancient school of philosophy which took it, in turn, from the Greek word for 'dog' (*kuon*) – because of their manners. The cynic either pulls down something lofty and noble to an everyday level, or sees the mean motive behind the noble act.

When a large number of girl-volunteers flooded Israel during the Six Day War, the sabra's comment was: 'They're only hoping they'll catch a husband.' German propaganda again proclaimed during World War I: 'The British will fight to the last breath of the last Frenchman.' Or Wilde: 'If a man is sufficiently unimaginative to produce evidence in support of a lie, he might just as well speak the truth at once.' Cynicism often belittles the great and attacks God himself. ('What a great country God could make of the United States – if He only had the money.') Take Wilde on the infinite Goodness of the Almighty: 'Don't you realize that missionaries are the divinely provided food for cannibals? Whenever they are on the brink of starvation, heaven, in its infinite mercy, sends them a nice, plump missionary.'[3]

The cynic makes fun of death; or he jokes about the downright horrible. Cynicism keeps tears away, which is why soldiers joke about impending battles, or ambulance men – otherwise not given to cynicism – about road casualties. Medical students joke during anatomy lessons, surrounded by corpses and dismembered limbs.

People enjoy joking about funerals, even about their own. A friend of mine – in his fifties – was told by a charming and much younger girl that she loved him.

'Not only for a few years, but to the end of your life.'

'Comes to the same thing,' was my friend's answer.

Some of the sick jokes are simply cynical. The mother calls out to her children who are playing in the churchyard:

'Children, what are you doing?'

'Playing with grandmother.'

'You haven't dug her up for the third time?'

Jokes about death and horror all show that the cynic is tough; that he can take it; that he is not afraid of things that worry the rest of us. But, of course, he is even more afraid; he is permanently preoccupied with the fear that he is joking about. Cynicism always has an element of cowardice in it. It is rarely the convinced atheist who tells cynical jokes about God or calls him by insulting names, but the agnostic, who is afraid lest God may, after all, exist and punish him; it is always the man who is afraid of, or preoccupied with, death who jokes about it.

The cynical joke is an attempt to tame a powerful opponent. The cynic tries to get on familiar terms with Death, or God, or Cancer, tries to make Death his chum; just a chap standing around the bar, enjoying half a bitter in his company; an amiable fellow, Death: surely he will not harm him. This is one way of taming death, of making it look less frightful.

Cynical remarks often hurt people. Religious people (particularly if deep down in their hearts they have doubts) resent dirty jokes about God; devoted monarchists (especially when they feel some lingering uneasiness lest the Queen be, after all, just an ordinary human being) resent jokes about the Sovereign, etc. Everybody has a borderline beyond which he will cease to see the joke and will protest or walk out in disgust. No one likes to do this, as the cynic is accepted as a sophisticated person and he will always try to show up the critic who resents his jokes, as an unsophisticated boor. Yet there is a limit to everybody's tolerance.

During the war, a friend of mine, a professional humorist and film gagman, was taken from Hungary to Auschwitz. He survived and returned to Budapest. When I saw him in the late forties, he was busy writing a *funny novel about Auschwitz*. He read to me one of his funny chapters in which he described – and very funny it was – how an S.S. man kicked some prisoners over a precipice. In between kicks three or four were allowed to pass; the author passed safely; now it was the turn of an enemy of his to pass and he watched, with bated breath, whether the S.S. man would kick him over or let him pass. He was lucky: the S.S. man kicked.

This author was trying to persuade himself that Auschwitz was quite an amusing place and he only went there to collect material for a funny book. He was no less terrified, of course, than the others when the S.S. man was making up his mind whether to kick him down to certain death. But, like everybody else, he had somehow come to terms with this frightful experience, to survive not only Auschwitz but also its aftermath. Some ex-prisoners (though not too many) reacted normally and time, plus the exercise of placing these events in perspective, has brought release, although not even the most normal among them was left without deep scars; some fall prey to melancholy, others carry a maniacal hatred for Germany – or all humanity – for the rest of their lives; others, again, became religious maniacs; heavy drinkers; or reckless gamblers: there are as many ways to react as there were victims.

My friend, the author, had to convince himself that all the horrors were just a joke – not to be taken seriously. The thought that ordinary human beings intentionally organized Auschwitz – that they really *meant* it – was unendurable to him. Perhaps this was madness but if it was, it was a mad reaction destined to preserve – or restore – his sanity.

(A footnote to this. I was firmly convinced that my friend's funny novel on Auschwitz never saw the light. But inquiries made after writing the above show that in fact it did. So perhaps I was wrong in stating that there was a borderline to *everybody's* tolerance. This novel, however, overstepped my own borderline of tolerance.

Or should I perhaps maintain that there *is* a borderline to people's tolerance but no borderline to their bad taste?)

What is true about kidding and wit and cynicism, applies with even more accuracy to the more complicated literary forms: satire, for example. Satire is also a way of aggression, a way of humiliating others and establishing the satirist's superiority. Even if the satirist does not state – or imply – that he could do better than his subject, sitting in judgment on others always implies superiority. *Candide* and *Animal Farm*, in spite of their charm and brilliance – and indeed, in spite of being masterpieces – contain a great deal of aggression and so does Swift's *Modest Proposals* (the suggestion that hungry Irish mothers should devour their own offspring) but here another element must be taken into consideration: *who and what are the targets of satire?*

The satirist is often a powerless individual whose only weapon is his pen with which he fights kings, tyrants and obnoxious political systems. Whether we agree with him or not, he deserves our admiration because of his courage. But, after all, the *Stuermer*, too, was to a large extent a satirical weekly which made fun of innocent Jews when – Streicher knew – they were being taken to the gas-ovens. The Russian funny papers also jeered at the kulaks while they were being executed in their millions (and a kulak in those days was any person disliked by the regime). I once heard (indirectly) jokes a hangman had told about men he had hanged.

When we talk about *sneer, sarcasm and jeering* we do not really mean that the joke, as a joke, is bad but only that it outrages our moral instinct so much that we refuse to examine its power to amuse. A *sneer* and *jeering* is a satirical joke we disagree with; a *satire* or *irony* is the type of *jeering* and *sneer* we approve of.

Most of the political jokes are satires in a nutshell. The Czechs told this story to each other after the invasion of Czechoslovakia in 1968:
Alexander the Great, Julius Caesar and Napoleon are watching the October Parade in Moscow's Red Square.
Alexander looks at the tanks and says:
'If I'd had chariots like these, I'd have conquered the whole of Asia.'
Caesar looks at the giant rockets:
'If I'd had such catapults, I'd have conquered the whole world.'
Napoleon looks up from the copy of *Pravda* he is studying:
'If I'd had a newspaper like this, nobody would ever have heard of Waterloo.'
Or another story about the credibility of Russia's great national newspaper.
In the course of his seminar, a party secretary explains that the little town of Novosibirsk was a heap of mud when the Communists took over. There was nothing there but ramshackle hovels, slums, muddy huts, no electricity, no roads, no sanitation. Today, there are skyscrapers, electricity and central heating in the houses, every worker has at least three rooms to himself, has a refrigerator, washing machine and television set. An old worker raises his hand and asks to speak:
'Comrade Secretary,' he says, 'I was born in Novosibirsk and it is absolutely true what you say about the old days. But I went back there last month and I can tell you, nothing has changed. There are still huts there, muddy roads, slums, no electricity, no roads and no sanitation.'
The Party Secretary shakes his head disapprovingly:
'Comrade, you travel too much and don't read *Pravda* enough.'
The first of these stories was told in Czechoslovakia, and the second – perhaps – repeated in whispers in the Soviet Union. But at the same time, jokes appeared in *Krokodil* and other Soviet papers, ridiculing the Czechoslovak 'counter-revolutionaries' and glorifying aggression and oppression. We find the Soviet jokes repulsive and the Czech joke funny, not only because our hearts are with the Czechs but also because we know that the Czechoslovak story-teller attacks the mighty and possibly risks his freedom by repeating the joke, while the Soviet joker is a journalistic hack, ordered to concoct jokes in support of the current Party line. We know that if he were ordered to reverse his jokes and attack his own former bosses, he would do so without batting an eyelid – as long as he knew that he was protected by the strong and powerful. Satire, in addition to its aggressive content, has this strong moral

content and no decent and civilized man can laugh at jokes aimed at people who are down and at people who cannot hit back.

Humour is always aggressive, hostile, and often cruel. So much so that it has been said that the savage who cracked his enemy over the head with an axe and shouted: 'Ha . . . ha . . . !' was the first humorist. William McDougall went as far as to assert that laughter has been evolved in the human race as an *antidote to sympathy*, a kind of protective reaction, shielding us from the depressive influence of the shortcomings of our fellow men. Humour is also an assertion of superiority; a means of humiliating others; and is often a reflection of cowardice. (Occasionally, as in the case of the oppressed who makes fun of the tyrant, it is a reflection of courage. On the other hand we have seen three types of cowardice in the humorist:

1 The 'don't shoot back, I'm only joking' type of cowardice of the court jester. In the same category we find the 'if you don't laugh, you have no sense of humour and you are a fool' type of defence.

2 The cowardice of the cynic who is so terrified of Death or something else, that he tries to fraternize with him, take him and make a boon-companion of him.

3 The cowardice of the satirist who, protected by the powers that be, makes fun of the poor, the weak, the down-trodden – in all cases the enemies of his powerful masters.)

In spite of all this, I have praised humour highly and in so doing I found myself in illustrious company. But some readers may wonder what good can possibly be left in humour if all the foregoing is true. Well, a great deal.

First of all, there is nothing wrong with a certain amount of aggression. Our forefathers – the cave-dwellers and hunters – could not have survived without it and even less could we, city-dwellers of today or citizens of the rural jungles. A fair amount of aggression is healthy; it is human. Well, perhaps it is animal, but it is still all right. Cruelty, on the other hand, cannot be defended; it is one of the worst crimes. But aggression canalized into jokes – even into the silliest practical jokes – is not the worst way of getting rid of a nasty (and healthy) impulse. If the choice is between knocking a man down, putting a bullet into him, breaking into a house, raping a woman, becoming a drug-addict, or making a pointless and silly joke, make the pointless and silly joke by all means. And who says that the joke must be pointless and silly?

Humour is aggressive and it is always aggressive. There is no such thing as an innocent and non-aggressive joke. (I have been trying to find some.) What about sex-jokes? Certainly not. Obscene jokes are a form of sexual aggression. Sometimes the most aggressively-worded jokes contain more understanding, even affection, than the seemingly milder ones, yet, they remain aggressive. (A woman was dug out from the ruins of her house during the *blitz* of London, having spent hours in the debris. She was asked: 'Where's your husband?' She replied: 'Fighting in Libya – the bloody coward.') It is the nonsense-jokes which seemingly come nearest to non-aggressive humour. (Two chaps meet. One says to the other: 'Didn't we meet in Newcastle years ago?' The other shakes his head: 'Never been to Newcastle in my life.' 'Neither have I,' says the first chap and then adds reflectively: 'Must have been two other fellows.') This joke is not aimed at any particular person, group or attitude of mind; but nonsense humour itself is aggression, an act of rebellion against the established order. Nonsense humour, with its modest and charming smile, is more aggressive, indeed destructive, than any other kind of humour. Yet, having admitted all this, we might as well add that the kidder, the teaser, the wit, the cynic, the satirist and even to some extent the practitioner of the sneer and the jeer, are all trying to find a *permissible outlet* for their aggression.

Humour, because it is aggressive, is a weapon, indeed a very effective weapon. If it serves a good cause, if it is aimed at the right target, it can be an admirable corrective or a great benefactor.

But, in addition to its aggressive content, a sense of humour also involves a sense of proportion. A man with a sense of humour will not think himself God and, most probably, will not even think God God. He may be a believer but his God will never be the wrathful, revengeful, ill-tempered, vicious and humourless God of the Bible but a good-tempered, understanding, humorous and rather humane Deity; a constitutional ruler. A man with a sense of humour will always be ready to joke about himself – and being able to do that is not just one insignificant trait. Indeed, humanity may be divided into two groups: those who can see a joke against themselves and those who cannot. The great, bloodthirsty tyrants of history were completely humourless: few people dared to tell Hitler or Stalin jokes against themselves and fewer still remained alive to wait for the laughter. On the other hand, some of the great democratic leaders – Churchill or John Kennedy – were witty men, often as cruel about themselves as about others.

Ninety per cent of the wars in history were fought for ludicrous reasons – millions of men have died for the greater glory of stupidity.

Diplomacy could not too often prevent a war from breaking out: but a sense of humour would have stopped *every* war in history, from the wars fought because of tribal feuds, wars over dogma, wars for dynasties, national prestige or bits of territory, up to the Kaiser's and Hitler's wars.

One curse of humanity is man's God-complex (as I said in an earlier work but, alas, I cannot claim to have gained too many disciples). Most people see themselves as Gods or godlike creatures. All little children want to be God when they grow up and many, by the time they *have* grown up, think that they have achieved their ambition. Wanting to be God is nothing but a human weakness: and God, as created by humanity, is nothing but the outcome of this weakness. A man with a sense of humour will regard himself only as a minor deity – unusual modesty on the part of any human being. Only a sense of humour can make a man see (more or less) his proper place in this world. Certainty and cocksureness are incompatible with a sense of humour. Humour means scepticism and doubt in *everything*: in *all* established values, virtues, habits, sacred dogmas and even facts; and first of all in oneself. It is scepticism and doubt which have been mostly responsible for progress. A sense of humour is maturity and wisdom; and there is no maturity and no wisdom without a sense of humour.

But what *is* a sense of humour? Many sages have tried – most of them unsuccessfully – to define *humour*; but few have tried to define a *sense of humour*. None of the psychologists who wrote about humour ever discussed, to my knowledge, the related notion of a sense of humour, and no philosopher has tried to define it. (Max Eastman wrote a book entitled *The Sense of Humour*; it is quite informative on a host of subjects except the notion of a sense of humour.) The Oxford Dictionary defines the relevant idea of *sense*: 'Quick or accurate appreciation of instinct regarding or insight into specified matter or habit (. . . the ridiculous, humour . . .)'. This definition tells us that a sense of humour is (a) instinctive and (b) an *appreciation* of humour.

A little Irish girl once told me: 'My friend and I have a marvellous sense of humour. We just sit down and laugh for hours on end without the slightest reason.' Few people will agree that this is really the apotheosis of a sense of humour. Most people would maintain that you must laugh at *something*. But everybody can laugh at *something*. The most idiotic story may be told and *somebody* will roar. An oriental despot may be amused at the spectacle of people's heads being chopped off. All of us, almost without exception, will laugh at the man slipping on the banana skin. I have said – and I am sure, rightly – that Hitler and Stalin had no sense of humour, yet these gentlemen did find certain things funny and occasionally even made jokes of sorts.

We may say that a man has a sense of humour only if he laughs at good jokes. But what is a good joke? This is only one way of saying that a man has a sense of humour if he laughs at jokes *we* laugh at. We, the speakers, are always men with a highly developed sense of humour. I have heard people admit to being criminals; to being cruel; only interested in money; wicked; immoral or mad. But only one man did I ever hear admitting that he had no sense of humour (and he was in fact a very funny man).

Some people try to distinguish between a sense of the ridiculous and a sense of humour. While this sounds convincing, it isn't really. Humour is often ridiculous; the ridiculous is often humorous. Others again distinguish between an active and a passive sense of humour: between the man who makes the jokes and the man who laughs at them. (The man who laughs at his own jokes, I suppose, is blessed with an active *and* a passive sense of humour.) It should be added that a man who laughs at the jokes of the others, who appreciates good jokes, has probably a better sense of humour than the one who makes bad jokes. Nevertheless, this distinction between an active and passive sense of humour still tells us nothing about the true nature of a sense of humour.

I shall not attempt a precise definition myself and I will say only this: Whatever else a sense of humour means, it must include the readiness and the ability to laugh at oneself. Everyone can laugh at *something*; only a man with a sense of humour will laugh at himself. There is nothing self-effacing in a sense of humour. Laughing at oneself does not mean that one is inferior to others; it means that we accept ourselves as erratic, foolish and bungling as all our fellow-creatures are. We simply grant ourselves a degree of humanity which we should probably lack without this ability to laugh at our own folly. To laugh at oneself does not mean to be modest, insecure, unsure. A man who is unsure usually takes himself deadly seriously and is given to watching himself anxiously at all times. If you are ready to laugh at yourself except on one or two points which are 'sacred' or on which you are 'certain' and tolerate no jokes, you are well advised to examine those points because they will cover your real uncertainties and doubts.

A sense of humour always contains an element of self-denigration, acceptance of one's own weakness. To see your own foibles, silliness, weakness, vanity, erratic nature and be genuinely amused by them is the true test of a sense of humour. The man who can only laugh at *things*, events, situations and other people has no sense of humour.

How do I fare myself?
I can laugh at myself all right but there is a dose of self-effacement in my laughter. I do not laugh at myself maliciously because I do not hate myself. In fact, I rather like myself, with all my faults. I am tolerant of other people's faults; but just as tolerant – if not a shade more – of my own.

I am not ashamed to confess this self-love, which is in no way (or perhaps just slightly) connected with self-admiration. I should, in fact, regret to have to confess the contrary. I like people and, after all, I am one of them. I do not revere myself; I am not terribly impressed by myself but I do like myself. I am not even biased: I like myself on merit. Many people would do well to try to love themselves more than they do. He who does not love himself cannot possibly love his fellows. The first commandment ought to be: Love thyself as you love thy Neighbour.

In other words, I claim to possess a genuine sense of humour and claim to have a certain amount of the wisdom that goes with it. But what about the darker side of humour? Its nasty and aggressive side?

I think I really fail to reach the heights I once aspired to as a humorous writer, because I am not aggressive enough. I see things in a pleasanter light than the truly great humorous writers can possibly see them. This is due to two factors: First to my dear and beloved mother. She was much too nice and much too sweet a person, gentle and protective; and like many others who had a pleasant childhood, I am trying to remain a child forever. It is nice to be protected by Mummy – this state of affairs suits me. I always believe that things will turn out well – because Mummy is there to put things right for me. So I am an optimist – and a great humorist must be a pessimist, a bitter and disillusioned man. The other factor I mentioned is my cowardice: a cowardice which, for long, I took for courage.

I have spoken of the treble aspect of the humorist's cowardice and my own rather worries (or used to worry) me because I should prefer to be grave and heroic.

Why did I become a humorous writer instead of, say, an aggressive revolutionary for which my dislike of authority might well have predestined me? I do, of course, have the humorous outlook: I see the humorous aspects of many things which others regard as tragic or indifferent, but I also choose to speak the truth – as I see it – in a comic manner because I do not dare to take it seriously. Like the court jester of another age, I want to protect myself against the wrath of my victims by the cry: 'I was only joking.' I know that public opinion also protects me; the man who takes a joke seriously is a stupid fellow, a fool, and the joke is on him, however deeply he may be hurt.

My writing is often a mixture of the serious and the funny. Readers occasionally do not know whether I am declaring something in all earnestness or with a twinkle in the eye. The rule is: if anyone gets angry, I claim to have been joking.

I have said once or twice before that I *wanted* to be taken seriously; that I *wanted* to make people angry. I said that the funny dress was only my way of going about it but, all the same, I felt like St George and was all set on fighting the Dragon. The Dragon never gave me the fight I wanted, or thought I wanted; he patted me on the back instead and said: 'Quite amusing.' I made out I was frustrated and disappointed – but I doubt if I really was. I always protected myself and tried to gain everybody – even my adversaries, even my victims – as allies. I hoped that if I, as a modern St George, did not kill the Dragon with my sword, ridicule – or the Dragon's fear of looking ridiculous, the Dragon's fear of being told that he has no sense of humour – would kill him or calm him down. I always wanted him to charge me – but I also wanted to be sure of my power. After all a man who can *hurt* is a type of tyrant, and we all want to be tyrants. If the Dragon had charged, however, I am sure I'd have shouted at him: 'Don't be a fool. Can't you see a joke?'

To sum up: I feel I am not aggressive, not malicious, not fierce enough to be able to aspire to literary greatness; and too cowardly to aspire to moral greatness.

But I can forgive all my weaknesses. I still like myself and forgive myself. And this tolerance is the most attractive trait of an otherwise not flawless character.

No laughing matter

Popular Fallacy No. 2: There are proper subjects for jokes; and there are others too sacred to joke about.

I have heard this many times. There is a vague idea that one may joke about mothers-in-law, maiden aunts, adultery, drunks, Jews, or commercial travellers in trains, and about all the funny things that happen to one on one's way to the Forum, but one must not joke about, say, the death of a child. This is nonsense. I do not say that it is legitimate to joke about any subject under the sun at any place and at any time but I do say that only the time and place are the decisive factors here, not the subject.

First of all, different people will regard different subjects as sacred.

Some time ago I was invited to a party in the house of a journalist friend, near London. The house was big and the guests were dispersed in many rooms. In one of them I was telling a homosexual joke to a few people. There was laughter when a fierce gentleman entered the room – the door had been standing open – and looked at me with fiery eyes.

'You told a homosexual joke,' he shouted at me in a stentorian voice. He sounded very angry.

'I did,' I admitted.

'A homosexual joke!' he repeated in a voice as if he had said: 'Murdering a child!'

'Yes,' I nodded.

'I am a homosexual,' he declared proudly, as if this had been a conclusive argument.

'I see . . .' I said vaguely.

'Yes, I am a homosexual,' he repeated with pride, much as someone might say: 'I have won the Nobel Prize in Physics' or 'I am a Hero of the Soviet Union.'

'So what?' another guest asked him.

This puzzled him. He repeated firmly:

'You made a joke about homosexuals and I am a homosexual.'

'But don't you see,' I argued, 'that one tells jokes about priests, rabbis, Jews, Catholics, Socialists, Tories, Americans and members of the Royal Family. Why should homosexuals be the one sacred subject under the sun one must never joke about?'

He went on to say it was boorish and uncivilized to treat homosexuals as figures of fun. I tried to point out that telling a joke about homosexuals is a far cry from treating homosexuals or homosexuality as a joke. I knew some good jokes about the Six Day War, I added, and this did not mean that I regarded the Middle Eastern situation as a frivolity. Indeed, did he not see that it was more important to joke about serious matters than about facetious ones?

No, he did not see this at all. For this man, homosexuality was the one sacred subject because it was the grave problem in his own life.

Few indeed would maintain that homosexuality is a sacred subject, immune from the joker. But what about death?

Death is a serious matter for the man who dies and for those who love him. But it is also part of human life, like birth, marriage, illness, adolescence and whooping cough. Man has joked about death ever since he was born – or ever since he started dying. Few people were outraged by the comedy *Arsenic and Old Lace*: the play – dealing with the murder of about a dozen people by two charming, well-bred and pious old ladies – was very funny and always in good taste. One of the humorous masterpieces of the century, Evelyn Waugh's *The Loved One*, is about Californian funeral rites and habits. Literature is full of funny deaths and amusing funerals; laughing at death gives us triple pleasure: (1) the pleasure of the joke itself; (2) the malicious joy of laughing at death's expense, and (3) the pleasure of taming Death and fraternizing with him (see the last chapter).

It is well known that one is inclined to laugh at funerals more readily, more loudly – indeed, more hysterically – than on any other occasion. This is caused by our desire to overcome fear and death, and has nothing to do with the question whether death is a legitimate subject of humour.

Jewish jokes – very good jokes as a rule – have been poking fun at death for time immemorial.

Two poor Jews are walking through a cemetery, looking at the magnificent mausolea – complete with marble statues and wrought-iron gates – of the Rothschilds and other millionaire families, and one of them exclaims enviously:

'My God, that's what I call high living.'

Another story:

Old Salomon is dying and his whole family surround his death-bed. He whispers in a barely audible voice:

'Is Rachel, my beloved wife, here?'

'Yes, dear, I am here.'

'Is Jacob, my elder son, here?'

'Yes, Father, I am here.'

'Is Benjamin, my younger son, here?'

'I am here, Dad.'

'And is Sarah, my only daughter, with us?'

'Yes, Father, here I am.'

The dying man sits up and asks in a loud and angry voice:

'If you're all here, who the hell is minding the shop?'

Or a joke about funerals:

It is Mrs Levy's funeral, and Levy is found in the maid's room, making love to her. The outraged relative who has found him exclaims:

'Today, of all days!'

Levy replies:

'Good gracious! In my great sorrow I don't know what I am doing.'

I mentioned above the death of a child as a legitimate subject for a joke, and this may have been thought too much by some readers. Max Eastman in his *Enjoyment of Laughter*, tells us that there was an early nineteenth-century tomb in a churchyard with this inscription:

Died April 15th
John, the son of Henry and Rachel Longbottom
Aged 2½ years

Someone had scribbled the comment on it:

Vita brevis, ars longa

It would be hypocritical to say that one is personally concerned about the poor little fellow, completely unknown to all of us, who has been dead for a century and a half. This joke is not only not offensive, but is also a good example of that rare bird, the witty pun.

For me the most abhorrent and tragic subject is a publisher who does not pay his author's royalties. Yet, my sense of humour seems so highly developed that I found even this story amusing:

A friend of mine, a good and successful Hungarian writer, was sent during the thirties to Sofia as a member of a literary delegation. Soon after his arrival, three Bulgarian gentlemen – all of them publishers and all three wearing morning coats and top hats – entered his room. Two of them did not speak a word of any language but Bulgarian, the third spoke broken German. This third man delivered a courteous, if somewhat flowery, speech about their association; the whole nation, he said, was greatly honoured by the famous man's visit, this was a red-letter day in the Bulgarian calendar and so on.

When this speech ended, my friend said – in German – that he was delighted to be in Sofia and the honour was his. There was, however, a small matter which had bothered him for a time, and his three visitors, being publishers, might he thought be able to throw some light on the subject. A large number of his books had been published in Bulgaria, all with success – yet he had never received one single penny in royalties.

The German speaker listened to him in deadly, stupefied silence. Then he translated and an excited, angry conference ensued, in rapid Bulgarian. At last the German speaker turned again to my friend and declared fiercely:

'Wir sind eine kleine Nation, wir zahlen nicht.' ('We are a small nation, we do *not* pay.')

(I told this story once to a colleague, who was a best-seller in the Soviet Union – and had received no royalties. He remarked wryly: 'They are a big nation; they don't pay either.')

What other sacred subjects are there? I heard the following story from a Roman Catholic priest who not only believed in celibacy but even practised it.

An Irish bishop visits a small village and is horrified to see that the parish priest has only one bedroom and apparently shares the bed with his female housekeeper.

'This is not so bad as it looks, my Lord,' explains the priest, 'we have a big board here which I put between us every night.'

'But, my son,' answers the bishop, 'what do you do if you are attacked by sinful temptation?'

'Oh, then? Then I take the board away.'

I have cited quite a few examples to show that jokes on any subject whatever can be utterly harmless and inoffensive. It is, indeed, the grand, the majestic, the impressive, the awe-inspiring, the redoubtable, which are, primarily, the legitimate subjects of humour: they must be tamed, humanized, cut down to size. Yet, obviously, there are many situations which do not exactly call for light-heartedness; situations in which attempts at humour would be outrageous.

This, however, has nothing to do with the subject, just with the place and time. You may joke about a dead child, 150 years after his death, to complete strangers, but obviously cannot do so to a recently bereaved mother.

I knew a young couple who set out on their honeymoon, and both of them died in a car accident a few hours after the wedding. To joke about honeymoons to their parents would have been unforgivable. The word 'honeymoon' sounded as horrible to these parents as the word 'Auschwitz' did to others.

The noise of laughter

Popular Fallacy No. 3: The louder
the laugh, the greater the amusement.

Laughter is an instinctive, physical reflex like sneezing and crying.
While very little has been written about sneezing or even about crying,
a whole library has been published about laughter. Yet, we know
considerably less about laughter than about sneezing. Perhaps if
another two hundred volumes were to be written on sneezing, we
would know as little about sneezing as we know about laughter.

We know that if we want to laugh we have to lift our upper lip, half-
close our eyes and emit a neighing sound. If we want to laugh violently,
we should also shake our body and lose our breath. On that people
agree – but on little else.

We may laugh at a good joke. We may also laugh at a bad one. A lot of
oriental people laugh when occidentals would cry or show anger. A
Japanese gentleman once told me that his house had burnt down and
his wife and one of his two children had died in the fire. And he
laughed. I was taken aback and for a moment the idea occurred to me
that his misfortunes had driven him out of his mind. Not at all.
Laughing at a sad story – a tragic story – is an oriental convention. The
teller of the story does not want to embarrass you – the laughter means
'I am going to get this shock over, I do not mean to ask for your
sympathy' and it certainly does not mean that my Japanese acquain-
tance found the death of his wife and child funny.

Another time in Bangkok, I saw a street vendor's cart knocked over by
a horse. All his cold drinks poured out, his bottles and glasses were
broken and the man, I was told, pretty well ruined. Yet he laughed
uproariously as if he had just witnessed the best joke of his life. He
had to, otherwise he would have lost face, he himself would have been
laughed at and that would have been worse than utter ruin. (A friend

who was with me on the occasion remarked: 'He laughs his head off. Then he goes home and commits suicide.')

What sort of reflex is this – we may ask – if a man is able to laugh at the death of his wife and child? Other people would surely cry at such a thing. And what sort of reflex is it that makes a man laugh facing financial ruin through someone else's fault? Other men – 'normal' men – would show anger. What sort of reflex is it if it can succumb to 'social conventions'? The answer is that these two men did not laugh *instinctively*; they produced or feigned laughter because a social convention demanded it. When the first man found out about the death of his wife and child, he certainly did not laugh, he must have been overcome by grief. He could feign laughter later. The second man could – and had to – laugh on the spot, but his loss, however grievous, was considerably smaller. Sneezing is a reflex; yet we may feign a sneeze whenever we feel like it. The fact that we can feign it does not prove that it is not a reflex when unfeigned.

You do not, however, have to travel as far as Bangkok or Tokyo to see that laughter and tears are closely related, indeed, often interchangeable. A man who has just narrowly missed being killed in an accident may first laugh with relief, and then cry with the passing of tension. After the lifting of any grave danger, people may laugh and weep alternately or even simultaneously. You say 'Boo!' to your baby. He is frightened – then he recognizes that there is no danger. He recognizes his father and he laughs aloud as the danger is lifted.

A joke may be sad. During the thirties there was a scramble for visas by German and Central European Jews trying to escape from the Nazis. Two of the Jews meet and one reports that he has succeeded in getting a visa at last.

'Where to?'

'To Australia.'

'That's very far.'

'From *where*?'

If the thoughts and sentiments expressed in this and similar jokes had been put down in a poem, it might be shattering and sad, a moving piece on the loneliness of man who – wherever he may be – is not near friends and human love and for whom the whole globe cannot offer one single friendly spot.

Laughter may be induced by many stimuli. If your sole is tickled with a straw, you will laugh; nitrous oxide – known as laughing gas – will also make you laugh; so will the electrical stimulation of a nerve, called the *zygomatic major*. Most of us have seen hysterical, uncontrollable laughter and I have also spoken of neurotic laughter, induced by the lifting of grave danger.

Simple euphoria – that nice light-hearted feeling – also makes us laugh. Some regard it as 'laughing without reason' and a sign of madness. But it *does* have its own good reason and perfectly sane and balanced people are capable of laughing because of euphoria.

We may ask: what is common to being tickled with a straw and being told a funny story – that both should produce laughter? Many people have asked this question and it has never been satisfactorily answered. But this need not concern us. It is sufficient to point out:

1 That it is not uncommon for various stimuli to cause identical physical reactions. Sneezing may be caused by a cold; by the same straw mentioned earlier; by inhaling pepper; or by sheer nervousness. Shaking of the body may be caused by cold; by fever; by laughter; by crying; by fright. (Everybody accepts these and many similar facts as natural, not worth explaining too laboriously; but the fact that laughter might be caused both by a straw and by an old Jewish joke, causes endless wonder.)

2 That we are here concerned only with the laughter generated by humour.

This will make our task simpler but not simple.

First of all, it will strike us that there are no clear-cut funny or tragic situations; there are no types of occurrences which make us weep and others which make us laugh.

Cohen, a citizen of Lemberg – then in Poland – goes to his friend, Green, and tells him that he suspects that Mrs Cohen is having an affair with Mr Schwartz. Would Mr Green be kind enough to keep Mrs Cohen under observation and report. Two days later they meet again and Mr Green gives his report to an anxious Cohen:

'Well, I was waiting outside your flat. I saw you leave after lunch, at 2.35, and precisely at 2.45, Schwartz drove up, parked his car right in front of your door, went up to your flat and came down, five minutes later, with your wife. They got into Schwartz's car and drove off.'

'Yes, yes,' nods Cohen excitedly.

'I followed them. I am afraid they did go to a small hotel and took a room.'

He seems reluctant to go on but Cohen presses him.

33

'And what then?'

'Well, to be quite certain, I took the room next door and looked through the keyhole.'

'And?'

'Schwartz started kissing your wife. This went on for quite a long while. Then he undressed and got into bed. So did she.'

'Yes, but what then?' Cohen prods him more anxiously than ever.

'They started kissing passionately again.'

'And then?'

'Well – then they switched off the light and I couldn't see anything.'

Cohen sighs, deeply worried.

'Good God . . . this uncertainty will kill me.'

That is how Mr Cohen reacted, because he is a comic hero. Othello reacted quite differently when *he* suspected *his* wife of infidelity. The difference is in the characters of Mr Cohen and Mr Othello – the situation is essentially the same.

Probing deeper into the matter will not help us much either. Bergson's book on laughter is regarded as a masterpiece on this subject but it is full of quite untenable statements on essentials. He states, for example, that only human beings laugh; that *homo ridens* is the only animal in nature capable of laughing. This is completely untrue.

'Although smiles and laughter are mentioned by several observers of orang-utang behaviour, no one has critically discussed the legitimacy of the terms. If they imply a sense of humour, one might hesitate to apply them. Yet, the abundant evidence of tricks, jokes and intent to surprise, tease or otherwise disconcert their ape or human companions would suggest even humour.'[4]

Everyone has seen horses, cats and dogs laugh and it is silly to say that they are not laughing at *jokes*. They are. It is quite possible, of course, that their sense of humour differs from ours. What is no joke for a man, may be a joke for a cat; a dog never laughs at a pun – which may prove the dog's superior sense of humour.

Bergson also states that laughter is a group activity and one never laughs when alone. But I often laugh aloud when I'm reading something funny and I once saw a girl reading a book on a bus, who had to get off because she was choking so much with laughter. People are also known to laugh by themselves when remembering a funny story. It is possible to say – and Freud said it about a different but comparable situation – that these people are only 'theoretically' alone. This is quibbling with words. A man who is alone, is alone. If we accept this 'theoretically' alone idea, then a man is never alone, and the whole contention of his being alone becomes meaningless.

Koestler said about some other aspects of Bergson's theory that, according to Bergson, the main sources of the comic are the mechanical attitudes of inertia, rigidity and repetitiveness impinging on life; among his favourite examples being the man-automaton, the puppet on strings, Jack-in-the-box, etc.[5]

'However,' Koestler goes on, 'if rigidity contrasted with organic suppleness were laughable in itself, Egyptian statues and Byzantine mosaics would be the best jokes ever invented. If automatic repetitiveness in human behaviour were a necessary and sufficient condition of the comic, there would be no more amusing spectacle than an epileptic fit; and if we wanted a good laugh we would merely have to feel a person's pulse or listen to his heartbeat with its monotonous tick-tack.'

In other words, Bergson, the brilliant and witty philosopher who wrote the most famous book on laughter, had a lot of confused ideas about it. Freud's theory is clearer: laughter occurs when repressed energy is freed from its static function of keeping something forbidden repressed and away from consciousness. Monro incorporates this idea into his own summing up of the three main theories of laughter which he says is caused either by superiority, by incongruity, or by release from restraint. He also mentions Greig's theory of ambivalence which, through proper and lengthy Freudian reasoning, comes to the conclusion that laughter is due to the *ambivalent* element in every joke. We nod: this sounds promising. But the inference would be that we laugh at mothers-in-law because our attitude to them is ambivalent. We are driven to the conclusion that our attitude to everything is ambivalent and, if this is true, then life is one endless joke.

If we turn to the great practitioners of humour, we fare no better. Voltaire thought: 'Laughter always arises from gaiety of disposition *absolutely incompatible with contempt and indignation.*' It is odd that Voltaire of all men should have said this, but he did. W. C. Fields said exactly the opposite: 'I never saw anything funny that wasn't terrible. If it causes pain, it is funny; if it doesn't, it isn't.' James Thurber took up a middle-of-the-way attitude: 'The things we laugh at are awful, *while they are going on*, but get funny when we look back . . . humour is a kind of emotional chaos told about calmly and quietly in retrospect.' [My italics.]

*   *   *

As I said before, if we want to read witty and thought-inspiring things about humour and laughter, we might turn to the *philosophical* literature dealing with them. If we want to find out what laughter really is (as we might try to analyse a novel, an international treaty or a quadratic equation), we will not get far. Our sources will not agree on what we laugh at; why we laugh; what laughter is. And if from our point of view it were sufficient to say – simply, primitively, but lucidly – that we laugh at funny things, even then they do not agree on what is funny and why it is funny.

The question we want to answer is this: if one joke is funnier than another, do we laugh louder at it? The difficulties in answering this are obvious in the light of the foregoing.

It might lead us further if we start from another angle: what is the difference between the smile and laughter? According to many psychologists, the smile is the outward sign of *love*. The first smile of an infant usually occurs after feeding – and it becomes associated with satisfaction, well-being and the mother's loving kiss. If this theory is true, the smile is connected with love, but it is not connected with the laugh. Psychologically this may be so; *humorologically* the smile and laughter are connected. The baby may smile after a satisfactory meal and, indeed, so may the adult. I have pointed out that euphoria may produce laughter, not only smiles. But the smile – like the laugh – may have several sources and we all know that if we are mildly entertained, we smile, if we find something excruciatingly funny, we roar with laughter. We also know that TV companies mix taped laughter into their shows in the hope that the ecstatic mirth will *prove* the success of their show. But does loud laughter really prove this?

Before I try to answer this question, I should like to say that laughter has been rather badly treated in recent years. People like to talk of it in a derogatory way. Laughter is supposed to be vulgar; loud, healthy laughter is stigmatized as the belly-laugh. The smile is the sign of true superior wit; people laughing loudly at a humorist, or at a comedy, are viewed with disapproval by the highbrow who thinks that only primitive people laugh loudly and only at crude jokes.

The truth is that good-quality highbrow humour may make you laugh, even roar with laughter. The reverse of this, however, is *not* true. Loud laughter is certainly no proof that you are laughing at something intellectually satisfying and truly witty (by the standards of the normal, educated person – if he exists).

I could laugh aloud at Leacock, Thurber and the Hungarian Karinthy – to mention only three distinguished humorous writers. But I only smile at E. B. White, Dickens, Chekhov (except the trial scene in *The Pickwick Papers* which always makes me laugh aloud) and at cartoons, however witty. Yet the satisfaction this smile gives me is complete, soothing and relaxing. Chekhov lifts me into a higher sphere and I enjoy my smile incomparably more than my guffaw at the man – or the clown – who slips on a banana skin.

But we all – or almost all – laugh at the man who slips on the banana skin. We are much too afraid of slipping on it ourselves, not to laugh. Yet – although the laughter is louder – no one will assert that the banana skin gives us higher literary or aesthetic pleasure than Chekhov.

But the television companies who mix laughter into their tapes are no fools. People *do* laugh at good humour and noise is audible and measurable, smiles and inner enjoyment are not. The loudness of laughter is misleading as a measure of *value*; but not as a measure of successful entertainment.

Because it is important to remember that people love laughing. Laughter, someone said, is taken as a sign of strength, freedom, health, beauty, youth and happiness. Whatever may be said about the inferior quality of some laughter, people still love it. The critic who praises a comic writer by saying that 'there is a laugh on every page' may upset the writer (whose aims may have been different) but he knows how to recommend a book to the reader. Highbrows might be right – from an aesthetic point of view – to condemn the belly-laugh – but people enjoy belly-laughs.

Philosophers – as I have said before – disagree about the causes of laughter. Some say (to mention the main theories only) that with laughter we want to demonstrate our superiority; others that it is due to incongruity; others again claim that laughter is caused by release from tension or by sheer aggressive instincts. Another school maintains that it is the playful streak in us that makes us laugh. It is possible, of course, that *all* these theories are true. We may laugh on one occasion because we feel aggressive; on another because we are struck by the incongruity of a situation and on the third occasion because of the playful element in our nature; or any single laugh may be caused by a combination of these and other elements.

Watching the man slip on the banana skin, or watching the victim of a practical joke, appeals to our most aggressive instincts and there is not much wrong in this: we *are* aggressive animals. We may be ashamed of our primitive instincts, but we shall enjoy the laugh. We may sit through a farce, laugh loudly all the time, yet, leaving the theatre, we may feel that the play was a bore and a waste of time: while we may read a Chekhov play, smile over it and be superbly entertained. The simple explanation lies in the diverse nature of laughter. The farce will appeal to the aggressive instincts, to the animal in us; Chekhov to our intellectual powers. Yet, all this must not make us forget that great humour may make us guffaw and a stupid farce may make us yawn. I feel the honour of laughter ought to be restored: we should not be ashamed of it; we should not call it vulgar and should accept even its aggressive characteristics, because we must accept ourselves as aggressive animals.

So – I repeat – loud laughter *may* be generated by the writing or the performance of a comic genius but even the loudest paroxysm will not prove that we are actually laughing at something morally or aesthetically satisfying and worth-while; but neither will it prove that we are laughing at low farce: a man falling on his bottom, losing his trousers or getting a custard-pie in the eye. We can never judge – merely by the decibels of laughter – whether it is the aggressive animal or the refined spiritual being who laughs in us. Most likely it will be a combination of the two. We can never separate them.

One final word about the confusion our philosophers, psychologists and other sages have caused by the constant mixing up of their notions and our motives. People do mix things up and this story will speak for itself.

Before the war, Jan Masaryk – later Foreign Minister of Czechoslovakia – was Czech Ambassador to the United States. He was invited to a dinner party given by one of the richest and most popular Washington hostesses. He went along with a Czech friend, enjoyed himself greatly and at eleven or so, got up to say good-bye to the hostess.

'Before you go, Mr Masaryk,' said the hostess, 'would you do us a very, very great favour?'

'Indeed, yes, if I can. What is it?' said Masaryk.

'Well, I know it's a bit of an imposition, but would you play us just a short piece on the violin?'

'With pleasure,' Masaryk agreed.

A beautiful Stradivarius was produced on a golden tray covered with purple velvet. Masaryk took the violin. He had learned how to play it as a child; he played badly, but he could play. Surrounded by all the other guests who listened to him with rapturous delight, he proceeded to play a Czech nursery rhyme. When he finished, there was delighted, uproarious and grateful applause. Masaryk was complimented profusely but he said it was really nothing and left with his friend.

In the lift, the friend burst out:

'What the hell does all this mean, Jan? All right, you cannot play the violin – why should you? All right, you played atrociously. But why on earth should these people ask you to play in the first place?'

'Oh, it's all very simple – don't you see?' replied Jan Masaryk. 'They have mixed me up with my father; they mixed him up with Paderewski. And they mixed the piano up with the violin.'

Who makes the jokes?

Popular Fallacy No. 4: Funny things
always happen to humorists.

This is a simple but frequent question which may be briefly answered. People keep reading about those funny incidents which supposedly make up a humorist's life. It seems to them that a humorist's life is an endless chain of hilarity into which worries, family disasters and income tax collectors only intrude in order to provide copy for yet another piece for *Punch*, while – they notice with dismay – nothing ever happens to them.

The truth is that funny things do keep happening to them. The majority of the funny things described by humorists in the first person singular have, in fact, happened to their friends, bank managers, business connections, who never noticed anything funny at the time. To describe such an event as if it had happened to the humorist is a simple device to increase the story's impact and make it more dramatic – a literary trick novelists use all the time. Indeed, the only essential difference between the ordinary non-humorous person and the humorist is that the latter notices the humour in all situations while the other misses it.

It was G. K. Chesterton who gave the perfect – and to my mind, final – answer to this question when he remarked, speaking of humanity at large:

'You make the jokes: I see them.'

My brother the clown

Popular Fallacy No. 5: All humorists
are sad, melancholy people.

Are they really? Before trying to reach the core of the problem, I can
make a snap survey of the humorists I know and decide on a quick –
and admittedly inconclusive – sample basis whether they are sad and
melancholy men or not.

Pierre Daninos, the distinguished French humorist, is probably nearest
to this popular image. A witty and entertaining writer, he gives the
impression of being a man of anxiety and tension, a basically sad man.
I remember one conversation between us particularly well. I was off
on one of my journeys and he asked me how I could find quiet and
secluded hotels to sleep in. I told him that I wasn't even looking for
such hotels, I took rooms in big hotels, in the centre of big towns, with the
traffic rumbling under my windows and the louder the noise the better.

'And you can sleep?' he asked me.

'Like a log.'

He thought this over and asked me again:

'You don't have, do you, a kind of Michelin guide, with a special list
for you of noisy hotels in the middle of towns?'

'I don't need a list. I find these hotels myself.'

He became very thoughtful for a while and then he told me:

'I bought a forest, miles away from human civilization. I had part of it
cleared and I built a house in the middle of the clearance. It is a cir-
cular house and my bedroom is in the middle of the circle, so it has no
outside windows – it gives onto other rooms. The whole house is
insulated against noise, and there is special, improved sound-insulation
in my bedroom. It has, into the bargain, soft, padded doors which are
fastened with clasps on the inside. There I lie at night with ear-plugs in
my ears. And I *still* cannot sleep, because of the noise.'

I thought it over carefully and told him:

'In this case, Pierre, you must be a little mad.'

'Yes, that's true,' he nodded. 'But still . . .'

I did not know James Thurber really well, but I met him on a few occasions. He was a man of great charm, and excellent company when relaxed; but he was shy and retiring, he gave me the impression that he tolerated his close friends but did not like other people. He was amiable, but mistrustful; generous, but slightly misanthropic. He wrote his best pieces on his family and childhood in Columbus, Ohio; indeed, to a great extent, he lived in the past and refused to grow up: a hall-mark – as I shall show later – of all humorists.

A well-known humorist with a world-wide reputation, whom I have known long and well, is Ephraim Kishon of Israel, formerly Ferenc Kishont of Hungary. He is a man who likes to be constantly reassured. Kishon is a man of outstanding abilities and I like him as a person, too. But while he can be aggressive and intolerant on occasions (he is a great Israeli chauvinist) he is certainly not a gloomy or depressed man. Stephen Leacock – a great humorist whom, alas, I never met but about whom I have reliable secondhand information – was a jovial and well-balanced man. He had his normal neuroses – and who hasn't? – but nothing worse than the average, normal, healthy man. If I come to think of one or two friends whom I know from London clubs or with whom I have worked – writers, and artists: Basil Boothroyd, Richard Gordon, David Langdon, Papas – I find them all pleasant and easy-going, more light-hearted and gayer of disposition than many writers of ghastly and nightmarish stuff – who, I suppose, ought to be mirthful and hilarious wags, full of boyish fun.

No one can prevent me, as the writer of these lines, from including myself in this illustrious company. I know from experience that the humorist does not differ basically from other human beings: when a disaster befalls him, he does not smile unconcernedly, whispering, 'How amusing!'

The Bajazzo figure – the white-faced clown – who cuts his funny capers while his child is lying dead – is one of the tritest sentimental figures of theatrical history. But as long as clowns remain human beings, they, too, will feel pain when kicked, the same pain as railway clerks or sanitary engineers, and when struck by tragedy they will weep the same tears as everybody else.

After a while I, personally, will see the funny side of tragic events (if they do have a funny side) and be able to smile at my own misfortune.

I do not think that anyone could describe me as a gloomy or melancholy person; indeed, I have often been described – critically, sometimes with scorn and often justly – as superficial, too light-hearted, one who is unable and unwilling to take things seriously. A man who always expects the best to happen, who believes that everything will turn out well, however black things may look at the moment; and a man who refuses to grow up.

This phrase 'refuses to grow up' takes us nearer to the understanding of the problem. But before I proceed further, I must make a few points clear.

I divide so-called funny men into two categories: humorists and clowns. Most people use the expression 'humorist' in a derogatory sense. To call someone 'quite a humorist' is not a compliment. Or put it another way: a man usually calls someone else a 'humorist', never himself. If, in turn, a humorist wants to decry a fellow-humorist, he calls him a clown. In other words: all humorists are inferior beings, but those called clowns are the lowest of the low. It is as with Negroes: all Negroes are bad, but the duskier the Negro, the worse. The clowns are the darkest members of the worthless clan of humorists.

The distinction between 'humorists' and 'clowns' is silly and pointless. Humorists and clowns indeed differ in kind, as I shall try to show, but they do not belong to an inferior race of writers, and the clowns – as a class – are not below the ordinary humorists.

The word *clown* is used in a derogatory sense by many people – not only by humorists, decrying a colleague. Describing a man as a clown, is as much as to say he is trying to be funny, that he is coarse, vulgar and altogether tiresome. If an actor in a comedy is described as 'clowning', the inference is that he is after cheap effects and is ready to drop his trousers to get a laugh instead of entertaining us by more subtle means. The circus or stage clowns, too, are regarded as the lowest type of entertainer: dressed in a uniform (which varies from one clown to another, yet is basically the same), red-nosed, white-cheeked with tousled hair, the clown is supposed to be the very incarnation of the coarsest and most vulgar type of humour. He is a stupid bungler, trying to be clever, trying to shine; but always he is frustrated, makes a fool of himself and falls on his behind. Sometimes we sense his loneliness; occasionally we wish him well – after all he is likeable – but then we shrug our shoulders and laugh at his stupidity and misfortune.

Even if this is the generally accepted picture of the clown, few of us would deny that there are some clowns of genius. Now, a genius is never

43

to be despised. Neither is it obvious why a clown of genius should be inferior to a mediocre humorous writer who tries to achieve his effects with subtler means, indeed, why a clown of genius should be inferior to a mediocre lyric poet, self-tormenting novelist or dull philosopher. And of course he isn't. A Chaplin, a Buster Keaton, a Grock or a Hulot tells us more about human nature, about our problems, about ourselves, than many so-called serious thinkers. A clown of genius simply chooses a funny way of telling us serious, often tragic things. Chaplin – the greatest of them all – shook us not only with his laughter but also with new insight while he was still wearing his baggy trousers and outsize shoes and still swinging his cane. When he started preaching his trite, sentimental and third-rate philosophy, he became not only less significant as an artist, *but also much less serious.*

So the description 'clown' is not in itself a value judgment. There are great clowns and small clowns, good clowns and bad clowns, just as there are good and bad novelists, violinists, physicians and surveyors. What is then common to clowns? And if clowns and humorists may be grouped together as 'funny men' – what is the difference between them? The clown is a depreciated father-figure, a man of authority deprived of his standing. He looks grand and is often cruel; like Father he tries to make us believe that he knows everything, that he can do everything but, in fact, he is only a fool, no better than us. He is not big and terrifying – although like Father, he wants us to think so – but he is feeble, ridiculous, incompetent, and just as much lost in this world as the rest of us. We are delighted to discover this: we are relieved and we enjoy our sudden glory; but he, the clown, is essentially a sad and melancholy figure. Every time he fights a windmill, he suffers defeat; time and again – whenever he runs his head against a brick wall, he discovers that the wall is hard and his head is soft; and – saddest of all – he realizes that he cannot really protect those whom he is called upon to protect.

Yet, there is a further essential element in our relationship with the clown: we love him. He is a Father: we want to see him humbled, ridiculed, brought down to our own lowly level, but we still love him. To hate Father would generate guilt in us and we could not enjoy his humiliation: we cannot laugh at the clown with an entirely clear conscience.

Remember Grock – one of the great clowns. He'd come on stage where his assistant – a well-dressed and well-behaved young man – was performing on the violin. Grock was huge, impressive, authoritative. He carried a vast suitcase of enormous proportions. He looked round sternly and pushed the young artist aside, opened his vast case – and carefully brought out the tiniest of violins. Loud laughter – authority deflated is always the best of jokes. The paternal figure carrying a huge bag which proves to contain only the tiniest of instruments, warms our heart, relieves our anxiety and reassures us that the luggage *we* brought on our journey may, after all, prove sufficient. But whether Grock was playing on his tiny violin, falling over backwards on the rebellious stool, or sliding down on the wooden keyboard cover (which he took out and leaned against the piano), we always loved him. He was not a stern, imperious father; he was our dear, silly Daddy. We were delighted to see him meet one misfortune after another and he entertained us sadly: he was resigned to his failures but he would have preferred to shine and to dazzle us, his audience, his children.

The humorist, on the other hand, is not a father-figure but a child himself – and a rather spoilt child at that. He knows of the miseries of the world but refuses to accept the facts that stare him in the face. He, as I have already said, is Peter Pan who resolutely refuses to grow up. Mother used to protect him and those were the happy times; so Mummy is still around – and always will be – and will go on protecting her baby. He is determined to see the world as a comfortable, rosy place, although at the bottom of his heart, he knows only too well that this conception is not quite accurate. Misery, danger, humiliation, failure do not exist for him; the world is a pleasant place and however dark something may look at the moment, all will turn out well. The humorist is a kind and jovial man, his world is a happy one; but he is far removed from reality and he knows that his picture is a distorted one. The world is the kind, tolerant, loving Mother, who watches her silly and unruly child with feigned strictness, but is always ready to forgive him and to embrace him with love.

The difference between the clown and the humorist is, then, fundamental. Both carry the seeds of unhappiness in themselves – so there is a grain of truth in the belief that both are gloomy and melancholy types. The clown tries to shine and keeps failing; the humorist refuses to see the darker side of life but suspects – or knows – that his picture is far removed from reality. The literary clown may write about himself or about a hero; Daninos's Major Thompson is a clown; Thurber – with his flights back to childhood – is a humorist. (No value-judgment, I repeat.) Both the clown and the humorist may be aggressive. The man who keeps failing might become very angry and frustrated; the wilful child who cannot have his own way might become equally aggressive. Both clowns and humorists are *likely* to be melancholy; both *might* be aggressive.

Yet, it is all a question of adjustment and deception. The clown may shrug his shoulders and accept his fate with resignation. The affection the clown earns, after all, compensates him, to a large extent, for his permanent misfortunes and lack of glory. Similarly, the question concerning the humorist is this: how well does he succeed in cheating himself into believing that this world is a pleasant place, that humanity is decent, that God – assuming He exists – is a benevolent deity and that all will turn out well in the end?

I am good at deception; I have succeeded in fooling myself perfectly. I am not a sad and melancholy man. *My* world is a pleasant world; the human species is a tolerable species – even if not altogether delightful; God, for me, does not exist, but if He did, He would be a lovable chap – not the wrathful and revengeful God of the Bible; in the end all will turn out well for me – even Death must have its pleasant aspects. Reality? There is no reality. There is only *your* reality.

Johnnie Papp

Popular Fallacy No. 6: If you
don't see a joke, you have no sense
of humour.

There was a popular figure in Budapest mythology called Johnnie
Papp. He was an actor but, I am afraid, he did not gain his immortal
reputation on the stage. He was immortalized by a comic weekly paper
and his name became a by-word in the Hungarian language much as
the names of Sandwich or Bowdler have become part of the English
language. Johnnie (or in Hungarian: Jancsi) Papp's claim to fame was
that he was passionately fond of telling jokes, but killed – indeed
massacred – all of them in the telling. Johnnie Papp, a kind and jovial
fellow, existed all right in real life and was still about in my time,
but, alas, I never met him. The weekly paper mentioned had a regu-
lar feature: 'How would Johnnie Papp tell it?' Even the original jokes
were perhaps not very good but the whole point was that any point
they had was lost in the telling – Johnnie Papp killed them all stone
dead.

Many a flaming matrimonial row has started by the wife telling a joke
and being interrupted by her husband: 'Darling, you are such a
Johnnie Papp . . . let *me* tell it!'

The idea was that Johnnie Papp, having no sense of humour, failed to
see the point of a joke. From which the general thesis seems to follow:
anyone who fails to see the point of a joke has no sense of humour.

We all know that tastes differ. As not all of us like the same play, or
film, or novel, we might legitimately differ about a joke, too. Appreciation of a joke is, after all, an aesthetic affair, like the appreciation of
more serious arts.

It is, however, possible to see a joke and yet fail to appreciate it. A
pious and devout person may see the point in a blasphemous joke, and
a devoted lover of the monarchy may see the point in a joke about the

Queen, but both will fail to appreciate these jokes or indeed concede that they are funny.

We often come across another and more interesting phenomenon: a bright person with an excellent sense of humour may suddenly fail to see a perfectly obvious point. This always has a very simple – or if not simple, explicable – psychological reason. Repression works in all fields and there is no reason why it should cease to work on the plane of jokes. The person who is precisely capable of understanding a joke and yet fails to do so, does not *want* to see it; he refuses to see the point because the point gets him on the raw. The point may, of course, be explained to him. He will realize what he has missed but will almost certainly shake his head and maintain that he still does not find it funny. That is why people say: you can never explain a joke, a joke explained is a joke killed. Of course, it never does a joke any good if it has to be belaboured. But the reason for the explained joke's unfunniness may lie elsewhere: it was rejected by a particular audience before it understood it.

On all such occasions some essential detail has been misconceived or overlooked.

Jacob Levine and Frederick C. Redlich, in their article 'Failure to Understand Jokes' (*Psychoanalytic Quarterly*, Vol. 24), give various examples to show how this mechanism of non-understanding works. They describe a cartoon by James Thurber which shows a little man going home to a very large house. In the background we see a furious harpy eyeing the little man with devastating wrath and it is obvious that a dire fate is going to befall him as soon as he enters the house. A competent, professional woman failed to understand this cartoon and even after questioning, she simply failed to see – actually to *see* – the terrifying woman who was the most conspicuous figure in the cartoon. The authors explain:

'This woman's hostile, competitive feelings toward men were held in check with difficulty; they caused anxiety and were often expressed by explosions of rage against her husband. Her blocking out part of the cartoon from her awareness seemed to result from a desire to avoid facing this conflict which was distressing to her.'

When the joke was eventually explained to her, she still saw nothing funny in it.

The authors give other examples: one person missed a huge dog in a cartoon; while another woman changed the sex of the person depicted. A woman was being burnt at the stake but she saw a man. Needless to explain that she *wanted* to see a man – her husband – burnt at the stake. It is possible that someone, hit by a joke, may yet see the point and is able to laugh at it wholeheartedly. I have praised such a man before, I shall praise him again. We are hit by the joke but, as psychoanalysts put it, our ego regresses, gives up some control and for a moment relaxes its jealous, guarding position.

This is really the ability to laugh at ourselves. We are able to let down our defences and laugh at our own expense. We *must* drop our defences to be able to laugh: he who laughs is defenceless; only he who is defenceless – at least momentarily – is able to laugh.

This is, in fact, the psychologists' explanation for self-irony. Another element – masochism – comes into it, too, and I shall have more to say about this when I analyse Jewish jokes. At the moment, I only want to point out that a great part of comic pleasure is derived from this very surrender. Some slight anxiety is always generated by our feeling defenceless but we are compensated because we know that the danger is not real, we may face it light-heartedly, we may laugh at it and if we laugh at one particular danger, we laugh at all danger.

The Johnnie Papp jokes were at a primitive level. There exists, however, a kind of joke which can poke real fun at the lack of a sense of humour; a non-joke may become a real joke. So-called aristocratic jokes were popular in Hungary at a time when aristocrats still more or less ruled the country. The jokes purported to show that aristocrats were silly and degenerate. (These jokes died a natural death after the war. There is no fun in kicking people who are down.) One of these jokes was about an aristocratic Johnnie Papp – Count Papp, I suppose. Someone asked him:

'How many sexual organs does a man have?'

'? ? ?'

'Three. His penis, his tongue and his finger.'

The Count laughs and when he gets to the National Casino (the aristocrats' club in the old days), he tries the same question on his friend, another Count: how many sexual organs does a man have?

'Three,' he tells his friend.

'How?'

'Well, his tongue, his finger . . . I am afraid I have forgotten the third.'

    *   *   *

So much for people who do not see the point, who are unable to appreciate a joke. What about the few who see jokes where the rest of us fail to see them?

A few months ago the man from the Electricity Board came to read my meter. I let him in, he opened the little box and read the meter. While doing so, he suddenly smiled. It was a knowing, worldly, nostalgic, perhaps slightly lewd smile which he tried to suppress as soon as he realized that I had noticed it.

What *can* be funny in an electric meter? What joke did this man see? If he can be entertained by electric meters, he must be a happy man; he must have the most amusing job in London.

Molnar's riddle

There are a few exceptional crafts which cannot be taught at universities. Journalism is one. Of course, a good general education is indispensable for a journalist who writes for an increasingly well-educated readership, but the stuff a young student picks up at a College for Journalists is almost useless. Journalism is a skill you learn during an apprenticeship, waiting in parliamentary or hospital corridors (or probably outside in the street), interviewing people, watching the fate of your copy, etc. – and not by passing exams at colleges. I said once that if I were an editor, the first requirement for a new recruit who wanted to work for me would be that he must not have a degree in Journalism. Perhaps I would insist on a degree; but if it was in Journalism, the candidate would not be considered.

Humour is another subject that cannot be learnt from books. The reading of humorous books can of course teach you a lot; but reading books *on* humour can teach you nothing – I mean nothing as a practitioner. Having read a whole library on humour, you may be much wiser and learned; but you will not make better jokes or more apt observations. You may help many other types of writers by teaching them the rules: dramatists, essayists, novelists, even poets; you cannot help the humorist.

Looking at these problems from the angle of a practising humorist, it might be worth while to return to the two most famous books on our subject: Bergson's *Laughter* and Freud's book on the joke.

I do not wish to attempt a precise analysis. Innumerable, better qualified people have attempted this and the result, in most cases, is boredom without enlightenment. I cannot succeed where so many others failed; but I can, at least, try to refrain from boring the reader, so I will simply deal with those aspects of the theory relevant for us.

Bergson's book is excellent reading – much better than the summaries. It is full of diversions and the diversions are the best part of it: entertaining, witty, brilliant. What he has to say on his main subject, however, is often downright silly.

Bergson's main ideals are elasticity, adaptability and the *élan vital*. The opposite of these, inelasticity and rigidity, are laughable – indeed, one definition of the laughable is 'something mechanical encrusted upon the living'. I have already quoted Koestler's remarks on Bergson's idea of fun: the man – automaton, the puppet on a string, Jack-in-a-box, etc. Koestler said, in effect, that if Bergson was right, Egyptian statues, Byzantine mosaics, epileptic fits, even other people's heartbeats, would turn our lives into perpetual merriment.

Bergson goes on to analyse all varieties of humour, to find that there is an element of inelasticity in everything that is funny. This is an intellectual exercise and our generation, used to watching Marxist ideologists performing on the flying trapeze, finds nothing extraordinary in this. Give me an attractive-sounding, apparently clever idea, and I will apply it to anything. It is an easy exercise and Bergson, of course, does it brilliantly. In the course of his reasoning, we find statements such as – all clothes are intrinsically ridiculous. He also finds physical deformity funny, if it can be successfully imitated. A hunchback, we are told, resembles a man who holds himself badly, so he is funny. A Negro is also funny because he looks like a man who has covered his face with soot. Bergson asks us: why do we laugh at a head of hair which has changed from dark to blonde? But do we? Personally I don't. He asks us: what is comic about a rubicund nose? Nothing, if he asks me. Why do we laugh at a public speaker who sneezes just at the crucial moment of his speech? Where lies the comic element in this sentence taken from a funeral oration: 'He was virtuous and plump'? It lies – Bergson explains – in the fact that our attention is suddenly called from the soul to the body. Any incident, we are told, is comic, if it calls attention to a person's physical qualities, when it is the moral side that really concerns us.

This is utter balderdash and offensive balderdash into the bargain. Physical deformity is not funny under any circumstances and it is painful to read that some educated people think it is. It's no good trying to fathom *why* a Negro is funny. He just isn't funnier than a white man and few white men are really funny; and when they are, it is not for Bergson's reasons.

He also says: 'An individual is comic who goes his own way without troubling himself to get into touch with his fellow beings. It is the part of laughter to reprove his absent-mindedness and wake him out of his dream.' There may be a great deal of truth in the suggestion that some of the great comic characters, like Don Quixote, were not adjusted to reality. But this is not to say that *all* of them are unadjusted, from the women of the *Lysistrata* to Bertie Wooster. And why bring absent-mindedness into it? Surely, absent-mindedness is not an indispensable element, except in those overworked professor jokes. Don Quixote may have been maladjusted; he was not absent-minded.

Bergson's worst failure begins with his doctrine that laughter is always corrective, intended to humiliate. So far so good; the aggressive, often unpleasant nature of laughter is not in doubt. But the deduction he makes from this assumption is that as a result of this it is impossible to laugh at oneself. It is indeed not only possible, but – for the very survival of the human race, it is necessary to laugh at oneself. I have said earlier – and I think rightly – that a sense of humour begins with one's ability to laugh at oneself. (See below – the masochistic character of Jewish jokes.)

One might suggest that Bergson – with his ideas that deformity and Negroes are hilarious, etc., is out of date. But he is a twentieth-century author – he died during World War II – and he has little excuse for being considerably more out of date than Aristotle.

Freud, in his book, refers to his predecessors. Fisher, at the end of the last century, thought that a joke is a judgment which produces comic contrast. He quotes Jean-Paul: 'Freedom produces jokes; and jokes produce freedom.' A favourite theory of the joke was 'the hidden similarities' which became unexpectedly apparent. 'Joking is the disguised priest who weds every couple.'

Freud's one point which I view with doubt is his *economy* thesis which I discussed in an earlier chapter. He gives us various jokes in his book: 'The girl reminds me of Dreyfus. The army doesn't believe in her innocence.' Surely there are more economical ways of calling a woman a whore. He tells us about two American businessmen of doubtful honesty who had their portraits painted. These were hung side by side, and when a famous art critic saw them, all he said was: 'Where is the Saviour?' Surely a witty way of calling the two gentlemen thieves; but an *economic* one?

Freud says that not *all* wit is aggressive and he distinguishes between *harmless* wit and *tendentious* wit. Harmless wit gives simple pleasure, tendentious wit a further pleasure, that of aggression and humiliation. In tendentious wit, the tendency is sex and aggression; the obscene joke is sexual aggression. He also speaks of cynical wit (which is often blasphemous) as a form of tendentious wit: cynical wit is always adjusted against a target. I think in here, Freud made a mistake: *all* wit is aggressive and if one examines the so-called harmless wit, one will find it pretty aggressive, too.

Freud also tells us that a joke is the most social of all mental functions that aim at a yield of pleasure. A joke, he says, often calls for three persons and the completion of a joke requires the participation of someone else. Jokes and dreams – he goes on – have grown up in quite different regions of mental life. A dream still remains a wish; a joke is developed play. Dreams retain their connection with the major interest of life; jokes aim at a small yield of pleasure. Dreams serve predominantly for the avoidance of pain or distress; jokes for the attainment of pleasure. But all our mental activities converge in these two aims.

When a humorist is determined to *learn* from philosophers – not only to understand his own nature but actually to *make* jokes – he finds himself in deep water. He feels like crying out and running away.

Koestler is perhaps the most explicit of all the sages. He says that a joke is nothing more than this. (See opposite.)

This he also explains in words as follows:

'The pattern underlying both stories is the *perceiving of a situation of idea L in two self-consistent but habitually incompatible frames of reference, M_1 and M_2*. The event L, in which the two intersect, is made to vibrate simultaneously on two different wave-lengths, as it were. While this unusual situation lasts, L is not merely linked to one associative context, but *bisociated* with two.'

This is, essentially, the 'hidden similarity' theory explained in a little more circuitous way. The poor humorist, who wants to learn how to make a joke, will find it bewildering. What is he to do? How to proceed – even *after* perceiving the idea of L in two self-consistent but habitually incompatible frames of reference? Just let it vibrate?

There is a story, written by Mikszath, a brilliant Hungarian novelist of the pre-1914 era, about a village blacksmith who was able to operate on people's eyes: he simply took a large knife out of his pocket – the same one with which he normally cut his onions, bacon and bread –

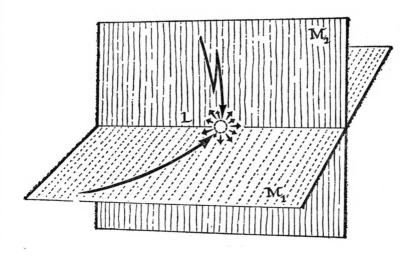

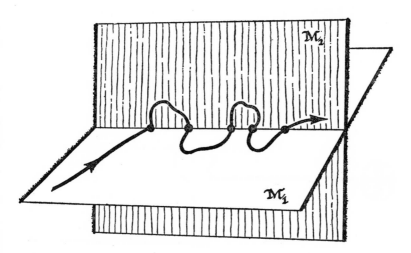

Arthur Koestler, *The Act of Creation*, pp. 35 and 37

and removed, for example, glaucoma. He never made a mistake and not one of his patients went blind. His fame spread and as the story sounded extremely improbable, a professor of ophthalmics at Budapest University took the trouble to travel up north to see the man at work. The blacksmith was as good as his reputation and the professor was flabbergasted. He asked the blacksmith afterwards if he knew anything of the human eye. 'No,' said the blacksmith; nor had he ever studied any surgery, or been a male nurse in the army. Then the professor praised him highly and explained to him *why* his feat was so out-standing: that he should find this and that layer without hesitation, remove this or that minuscule spot with absolute precision while a mistake, amounting to a fraction of a millimetre, would blind the patient for ever. The blacksmith nodded and was deeply impressed: he had never known what a dangerous act he was performing. He had just walked the tight-rope with natural skill and courage, never once looking at the depths underneath. But once the professor had explained all about the pupil, the iris, the retina, the coloured haloes, eyeballs, and fractions of millimetres, he became self-conscious, his hand trembled and he was never again able to perform an operation.

What Koestler says about the anatomy of humour may be true for all I know; but if any humorist, while writing something funny, were to start thinking, if he succeeded in making the habitually incompatible frames compatible, not only would the events vibrate but also the humorist's hands, too – as the hands of the blacksmith, after the explanation.

We also have this figure in Koestler's book two pages later. (See opposite.) This is a much better joke.

According to Max Eastman this is a joke:

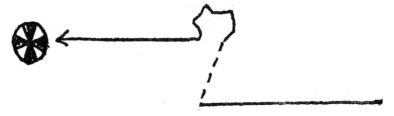

Max Eastman, *The Enjoyment of Laughter*, p. 351

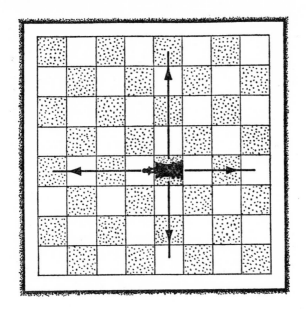

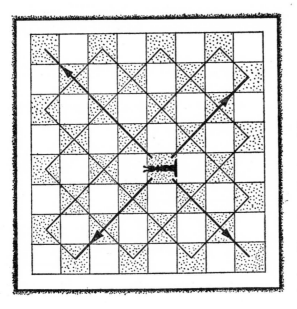

Arthur Koestler, *The Act of Creation*, p. 41

But, without wishing to be discourteous to Mr Eastman, I find Mr Koestler's jokes funnier.

Koestler, however, in his book (*The Act of Creation*), raises humour on to a new pedestal. According to him, the jester is a brother of the scientist and the artist. Comic comparison – humour – is intended to make us laugh; objective analogy – science – to make us understand; poetic image – art – is to make us marvel. Creative activity – he goes on to say – is trivalent: it can enter the service of humour, discovery or art. Or, put it differently. One branch of the creative activities is humour. The jester is the brother of the sage – and we, jesters, must indeed be grateful to such a distinguished authority for such a compliment.

Yet, after all this, and after all our previous studies, we must rest content with the idea that humour contains certain basic elements (aggression, a desire to humiliate, a desire to shine at someone else's expense, sheer malice, etc.); it also has a great deal of more attractive elements (a sense of proportion, a modicum of wisdom, an inclination to put ourselves in our proper place in this world) but the rest – the nub of the problem – must remain a mystery.

Ferenc Molnar, the great playwright and equally great connoisseur of good coffee, said once after drinking a cup of the suspicious-looking black liquid which was available in Budapest after the First World War:

'It contains one good thing, one bad thing and one mystery. The good thing is that it contains no chicory; the bad, that it contains no coffee; the mystery: what makes it black?'

I feel the same about humour. It contains good things, bad things and mysteries. And I am quite prepared to leave it at that.

Part 2   The joke as minor art

The joke as minor art

Is there such a thing as a national humour?

A Swiss delegation reports at the Pearly Gates and tells St Peter that they wish to see God. They are led to the presence of the Almighty and the leader of the delegation hands over a huge and altogether superb piece of cheese – a whole wheel of it. God asks what this is for. The leader explains: this is the way the Swiss wish to express their gratitude to the Creator for having made their country so beautiful, so wonderfully attractive and so prosperous. They also want to thank God for all those tourists who make them rich.

God nods and thanks them for their kind words. He expects them to leave, but they do not move.

'Well,' says God, 'is there anything else?'

'Yes, Almighty,' replies the leader of the delegation, 'the price of the cheese is 37 francs 50 centimes.'

This may be quite a nice little story but it tells us little about Swiss national humour. It is a joke *about* the Swiss, perhaps in a mild and not too hostile way, even a joke *against* them. But as likely as not, it was not invented by the Swiss. It is a thumbnail sketch of a certain Swiss habit as seen by critical, but not too unfriendly foreigners. Like caricatures, it tells us something about the Swiss, but does not reflect their own sense of humour.

The same remarks would be less true about Scottish jokes – all of which turn on the alleged meanness of the Scot. These jokes arose from a misunderstanding: the Scots were poor but not mean: very careful with money in a country where, not so very long ago, sixpence was a considerable sum. Extreme care about money and appreciation of tiny sums – which seemed ridiculous to the better-off English – could easily be taken for meanness. But it was not.

So the question still remains whether there is such a thing as a national humour. Humour is a manifestation of national character. If there is national character, there is national humour. But is there national character? Is any trace left of it?

There is a peculiar two-way traffic in this field – rather a curious phenomenon. On the one hand, national characteristics disappear, regrettably and rather quickly. While differences in speech are still very much in evidence in Britain, BBC English has made an enormous impact in the last few years. All over the world more and more people read the same newspapers, see the same comic strips, watch the same television shows and laugh at the same jokes. Differences in education remain but they, too, get narrower. Yet it is probably true to say that educated people all over the world laugh at the same things; and perhaps the same is true of uneducated people. On the night of my arrival in Japan in 1957, I saw a large, silent crowd on a bombed site. When I asked a Japanese friend what they were doing there, he told me they were watching television. He explained to me that the commercial television companies wanted as many people as possible to see their advertisements, so they put television sets in public places – such as bomb sites – where people could watch free of charge. The idea of seeing my first Japanese television show intrigued me, so I got into the crowd and spent about half an hour moving slowly nearer, until I could see what was on the screen – and what this silent, solemn and serious crowd was actually watching. It was the *I Love Lucy* show.

(The absence of laughter, by the way, did not prove that the show was a flop with them. The Japanese – as I said before – may laugh at the death of their parents but not at the *Lucy* show.)

So we witness a peculiar phenomenon. On the one hand, frontiers expand: the Common Market, EFTA, various federations, confederations, or looser ties – such as the Organization of American States, the Caribbean Federation, the United Arab Republic and the Union of Arab Emirates, come into being. The world seems to realize that it is growing smaller, so larger units are required. The frontiers of the mind seem also to be expanding: ideas, science, scholarship, are all becoming more international and, as I have remarked, more and more people are looking at the same strips and watching the same television programmes But the opposite trends are also noticeable: people, just because they feel the whole of humanity is being smothered in the same universal and tasteless sauce, make desperate efforts to keep their identity. The Caribbean Federation has broken up; some others don't really work. Small islands, like Jamaica, Malta and Cyprus, become independent, and even Anguilla – with its 6,000 inhabitants – has had a go. Cyprus, as if it were not small enough as it is, fragments into further Greek and Turkish sectors. Scottish and Welsh nationalism is aflame and someone explained to me a few days ago that the people of South Wales are really a race apart from the people of North Wales. The tendency is still to become tasteless, colourless and uniform; what we are witnessing in a few small countries is not an inexplicable contradiction but desperate, praiseworthy and doomed rearguard actions.

But, at the moment, there still *are* jokes which reflect the national sense of humour and thus the national character.

I have always thought that this little story is typically English:

Two men are standing on the platform of Aldgate East underground station – two Cockneys, as they inevitably must be in Aldgate East stories – at 11.30 at night. There is only one other person there, at the other end of the platform.

'D'you know who that chap is over there?' asks one of the men.

'Who?'

''E's the Archbishop of Canterbury.'

'Don't be a fool.'

'I tell you, he is. He is the Archbishop of Canterbury.'

'Look here, Bert, what would the Archbishop of Canterbury be doing at half-past eleven at night, waiting for a train at Aldgate East station?'

'I don't know *what* he would be doing here, but I've often seen his picture, and it's 'im all right.'

'I bet you anything 'e ain't the Archbishop.'

'How much?'

They bet a pound and Bert walks over to the other man and speaks to him:

''Scuse me but do you happen to be the Archbishop of Canterbury?'

'Am I who?' the man asks darkly, and does not seem at all amused.

'The Archbishop of Canterbury.'

'You —— off, but quick. Mind your own business and go to f—— hell.'

Bert walks back to his friend and says:

'The bet's off. You can't get a straight answer out of him.'

Why is this joke so English?

First of all, take the nonsensical conversation between the two chaps. Anywhere else they would quarrel, they would be rude: here we have just a comparatively courteous dispute. Bert tries to resolve the dispute in a simple and pragmatic way: "Scuse me, sir, but do you happen to be the Archbishop of Canterbury?' After the rude rebuff, we come to the sham fairness. The British are, of course, basically fair – at least an average Englishman *means* to be fair. The odd Englishman may steal, rob, cheat, but even the average British thief tries to be fair. To steal, or to break into a house is one thing: what do you expect from a professional criminal? A man has to live. But to be unfair, that is a stigma he refuses to bear. In a country in which fairness is at such a premium, we have a lot of sham-fairness too, the point being that even the most cunning crook wishes to *seem* to be fair. Bert knows that the man is not the Archbishop of Canterbury because His Grace would be most unlikely to use such language. But instead of coming back to say, 'Well, chum, I've lost,' he calls the bet off with an air of public-school fairness. In Jewish jokes the cheat is always superbly clever; in German jokes the victim is extremely stupid; in English jokes he is just fair.

Or, take another story:

Smith meets his old friend Brown and tells him he has decided to get married.

'Who's the girl?'

'Jane Huggins of Camberley.'

'Are you mad?' asks Brown, astonished.

'Do you know her?'

'I do know of her. And so does everybody else in the district. She has been in bed with half of Camberley.'

Six months later they meet again and Smith tells his friend that he is married.

'Who's your wife?'

'Jane Huggins of Camberley.'

'But how *could* you?' exclaims Brown. 'Didn't I tell you that every other man at Camberley had been in bed with her?'

'Yes,' says Smith, 'but afterwards I went to Camberley and – well, it's quite a small place.'

I think this is a very English joke, too. We see the motives of fairness once again: an Englishman is cool, judicial, and makes up his mind according to the merit of the case. Self-depreciation comes into it, too. The Englishman likes telling jokes against himself: the hero (or should we say subject?) of this joke is engagingly silly and honest and that is the image the Englishman likes to have of himself. This is the explanation for the immense popularity of the Bertie Wooster type of hero: an Englishman does not *like* to be clever. Clever is a word of abuse here: the true Englishman prefers to be stupid because – according to his notions – a stupid man *must* be fair and honest. The Englishman is also *pragmatic* – never theoretical. An Italian or German would reject the girl after Brown's information. The Italian because he insists on a virgin; the German because he has 'principles', he has theories. If a woman has slept with half the town, she is no good. But the pragmatic English mind knows that it is not only the woman he has to judge; it depends also on the size of the town. And, of course, it does make a difference whether someone has slept with half of Camberley or half of Birmingham.

The streak of self-depreciation is an important element in this story and this makes it not only attractive but also typically English. If this joke were a Jewish one, Smith – or rather, Cohen – would have gone to the *schadchen*, the marriage-broker, and *he* – Cohen – could have objected to the girl on the grounds mentioned and it would have been the *schadchen* who would have pleaded: 'But it's quite a small town, after all.' The Jewish joke would be different not because the Jews are incapable of self-irony (they outdo even the English at it) but because they reject the idea that they themselves are stupid. The hero of an English joke may be – almost ought to be – silly; the hero of a Jewish joke (the marriage-broker, in this case) must be sly and clever. I think a true conversation I described in an earlier book reflected a typically American mentality. I met a dairyman somewhere in the more obscure streets of Manhattan and started a conversation with him. One of the first questions he asked me was this:

'Are you Jewish?'

And before I could reply, he told me:

'*I* am Jewish. And proud of it.'

'Why?' I asked the man.

'What do you mean *why*? Why am I Jewish?'

'No. Why are you proud of it?'

'But I have always been proud of it.'

'Very well. But that still doesn't explain *why* you are proud of it.'

He was puzzled. Apparently no one had ever asked him this question before. He grew suspicious:

'What a funny question to ask. Are you an anti-Semite, or what?'

'I am just wondering why you are proud of being Jewish. Or why should one be proud of being an American, a Turk, an Englishman, an Eskimo, or anything. Surely, it's all right whatever you are – you were born that way. But it's not an achievement. Why are you proud?'

He thought this over for quite a time and was obviously relieved to find out that I did not mean to insult him. In the end he replied:

'I reckon it's this way. I am proud of being a Jew because if I wasn't proud I'd still be a Jew.'

I like this remark. It reflects a naïve and rather endearing pride but there is nothing pompous or offensive about it. It is funny and very American to start a conversation by asking a perfect stranger the question: 'Are you a Jew?' Of course, it's not simply that the very first question concerns some rather personal, private matter. It would not be funny at all if someone asked another chap in London: 'Excuse me, sir, are you a Lutheran?'

The Jewishness has a funny, twinkle-in-the-eye undertone in New York because American humour – certainly New York humour – at its best – is Jewish humour; New York humour is an innocent Jewish conspiracy. In New York the Jewish spirit prevailed by sheer numbers. New York is the biggest Jewish city in the world; there are more Jews in New York than in Tel Aviv or Jerusalem, more indeed, than in the two cities put together. Besides, there were other factors which helped Jewish humour to flourish: there was just the right mixture of freedom and oppression. America was – and is – a reasonably free country, so the Jews could prosper financially, could criticize conditions and open their mouths if they desired to do so. Yet, Jewish humour needs a certain amount of oppression as well and The Land of Hope and Glory supplied this need too. Jews in America were always made to feel that they were in an Anglo-Saxon land – which, of course, America isn't. Even the so-called Anglo-Saxons, while they have many admirable characteristics, are often snobbish, snooty, arrogant and stupid – in other words excellent targets for jokes. As a result, most of New York's great comedians – from the Marx Brothers to Mort Sahl – and quite a few of its humorous writers – from Bemelmann to Perelman – are Jews. But even the non-Jews – even the most American among them – are more Jewish, more integrated with or infected by the spirit of Jewish humour, than they care to admit.

What is typically American – not Jewish, but American – is the over-statement. An astonishingly fast-growing country impressed even its builders; they performed miracles but no one admired these miracles more than they themselves. This miraculous growth favoured the habit of overstatement and wild exaggeration. I quote an example or two from P. G. Wodehouse, an Englishman if ever there was one, but an Englishman very popular in America, perceptive to American humour and who has lived there for many years.

There is one single, solitary snake in someone's bedroom, but the hero finds it 'infested with snakes'. There is one solitary girl in Bertie's cottage at night but he complains of 'every nook and cranny bulging with blighted girls'. When Blashford Braddock wants to impress Osbert Mulliner, he tells him, among other things, that in Central Africa he strangled a jaguar with his bare hands. He adds: 'I had a rather tricky five minutes of it at first, because my right arm was in a sling and I could only use my left.'

Having quoted one of the most English humorists as a prototype of American humour, let me quote a very American author on the English, as a further example of something typically American. Ogden Nash wrote in his *England Expects* – still in days of the British Empire:

> Englishmen are distinguished by their traditions and ceremonials,
> And also by their affections for their colonies and their con-
> descension to their colonials.
> When foreigners ponder world affairs, why sometimes by doubts
> they are smitten,
> But Englishmen know instinctively that what the world needs most
> is whatever is best for Great Britain.

And further down in the same verse:

> England is the last home of the Aristocracy, and the part of
> protecting the aristocracy
> from the encroachments of commerce has been raised to quite an
> art;
> Because in America a rich butter-and-egg man is only a rich
> butter-and-egg man or
> at most an honorary LL.D. of some hungry University, but in
> England, why before he
> knows it he is Sir Benjamin Buttery, Bart.

I have quoted these Nash lines mainly in an effort to bring out the grotesque charm of American humour. American humour is, in fact, much more grotesque than ours – a great point in its favour – and Ogden Nash's dead-pan charm, wit and engaging drollness is one of the best examples of it.

67

In a fast-growing, fast-shooting society, impressed by things *done*, the practical joke has found a fertile soil. There are admiring and approving books written on practical jokes and jokers but admiration for them is not universal. To quote Ogden Nash once again:

> There is at least one thing I would rather have in the neighbourhood than a gangster,
> And that one thing is a practical prankster.
> I feel that we should differ more sharply than Montagues and Capulets or York and Lancaster,
> Me and a practical prankster.

There is a further type of American joke which should be mentioned. I could find dozens of invented examples but I shall quote a conversation I overheard in Jerusalem's King David Hotel – and quoted in my book, *The Prophet Motive*. I was sitting in the hall of the hotel and next to me there was an American couple, ready to depart, waiting for their taxi. The husband said:

'You know, Jean, this is really terrible. We've promised Mabel to go and see Tiberias, and here we are on our way back without having seen it.'

'What's so terrible in that?'

'Well, we *did* promise.'

'I know we did,' said the lady, 'but we did see it.'

'We didn't.'

'We did.'

'Tiberias?'

'Sure.'

The man shook his head: 'Never. You are pulling my leg.'

'Well, Jack, do you remember the place we had that very tough steak? You said you'd never had a tougher steak in all your life.'

'I sure remember that.'

'Well, that was Tiberias.'

This type of joke, however, is not an American joke, it is an anti-American joke. Americans are not 'like that', but quite a few of those American Vice-Presidential types, seen through European eyes, are exactly like that. This joke belongs to the same category as the Swiss joke, quoted at the beginning of this chapter. It may be characteristic of some Americans; but it isn't really American humour.

I have read in a book that one peculiarity of American humour is the understatement. This is utter nonsense, indeed the opposite is the truth. The author has read something about understatement and he tried to apply his knowledge. Understatement is not only a typically English characteristic but, as I shall explain in a little more detail in the next chapter, also part of the English air; it is a way of life. If America has any atmosphere of her own, it is a teasing, kidding, leg-pulling type of humour which I find very tiresome. The joker is always on his guard, tries to be funny, without respite, tries to show his superiority, tries to shine. There is something irritating and adolescent in this permanent kidding and the better-educated Americans dislike it as much as Europeans do.

An Italian joke:
Two gentlemen meet in Britain and one is delighted to discover that the other is a compatriot of his.
'You Italian?' he shouts with delight.
'Yes. Me Italian.'
'That's wonderful. Me Italian too. What's your name?'
'Luigi.'
'Luigi? . . . How nice. Me Luigi too. Luigi what?'
'Luigi Ratti.'
'Incredible! Me Luigi Ratti too. Which town do you come from?'
'Perugia.'
The first man is quite frantic.
'Marvellous! . . . You Luigi Ratti, Italian from Perugia – and me too, Luigi Ratti, Italian from Perugia. How do you sign your name?'
The other takes a pencil and a piece of paper and puts his signature on it: XXX XXX.
The first man nods.
'And how do *you* sign your name?' he asks.
He takes the pencil and writes: XXX XXX xx.
The other examines it in some surprise.
'I see . . . XXX for Luigi; XXX for Ratti. But what are the two little ones at the end?'
The other shouts:
'DOTTORE!'
This isn't just a story about pretentious ignorance; indeed, it is not about pretentious ignorance at all. It is *Italian* because it reflects the great joy of meeting another Italian. The Italians love their family and, once abroad, all Italians belong to the same big family. The joke is also

very Italian, because there is much naïve pride and showing-off in the conversation, and the childish snobbery is pricked in a most amusing way. It is devoid of the malice found in most other anti-snobbery jokes.

A German joke:
A man, a foreigner, Central European, with some vague knowledge of German, walks along the streets of Berlin and stops a very Prussian policeman.
(This is obviously a pre-war joke; not only the land of Prussia but also the notion of a Prussian got extinguished after 1945.) He asks the policeman:
'Excuse me, where is Kaiser Wilhelm Strasse?'
The policeman tells him in quick-fire staccato:
'Straight ahead, turn right at the church, walk along to the third set of traffic lights, then left, then at the bookshop left again, pass the Post Office, then first left, third right, and second left again.'
The man, dazed, mutters meekly:
'Thank you.'
The policeman looks at him:
'Nicht danken. Wiederholen!'
('Don't thank me. Just repeat it!')

And just one Jewish joke here, also about asking your way in a town. Cohen walks along the street in Tel Aviv, carrying two huge water melons. Someone stops him.
'Where is Ben Yehuda street?'
Cohen answers:
'Please hold these two water melons.'
The man takes them, whereupon Cohen makes an expansive gesture with his hands and says:
'I don't know.'

A remark of La Fontaine's may serve as a typical manifestation of French humour. He was asked if he had ever wanted to marry. He replied:
'Sometimes in the mornings.'

This was obviously a reference to early morning erections (someone told me once that Frenchmen had early morning erections, Englishmen early morning cups of tea) and the remark was supposed to be typically French because it is witty *and* cynical: it reduces marriage simply to a way of fulfilling a very ordinary physical need.

If, after all these stories and examples, we put the question again: well, is there a national humour, we are able to give an answer, with some reservations.

Most of the jokes are crude in a way. They are not bad jokes at all, but as mirrors of the national character they are not very subtle. But we were looking for typical national jokes and something *typical* cannot be subtle. A typical story is bound to use broad lines.

National characteristics, however, do exist, and a national humour is a reflection of these characteristics. As long as there are national characteristics, there will be national humour, too. This may not be for long. Education is spreading and life is becoming more and more uniform and international. This argues badly for national humour – but national humour has its own traditions and is not on its death-bed yet.

Understatement

A friend of mine, a brilliant musician and a great expert on national music, used to say that there were three truly national types of music in Europe: the Russian, the Spanish and the Hungarian. It is not that these are better than others; not that *any* Russian folk song is nicer than – say – a Danish folk song; it's not that a Hungarian *Csardas* is better music than German *Lieder*; but it is true if you hear a Russian, a Spanish, or a Hungarian theme there is no mistaking it.

Similarly, there are only a few outstanding characteristics of national humour worth discussing. Before I come to self-mockery in a later chapter, I want to say a few words about a British – perhaps English – trait – the understatement, which is as distinguishable from all other types of humour as a Spanish *flamenco* is from a Schubert *Lied*.

I have quoted Wodehouse – perhaps the most English of humorists – as an example of the American overstatement, so it is only fair that I should quote him now, when I am discussing this most English of humorous phenomena.

When Cedric Mulliner tries to escape from a compromising situation through the window, the window-sash descends on the back of his neck like a guillotine and he finds himself firmly pinned to the sill. What can he do? He thinks his situation over.

'His thoughts,' Mr Wodehouse explains, 'as may readily be imagined, were not of the most agreeable. In circumstances such as those in which he had been placed, it is but rarely that the sunny and genial side of a man's mind comes uppermost.'

Understatement is also under-reaction. Also from Wodehouse:

'Have you seen Mr Fink-Nottle, Jeeves?'

'No, sir.'

'I am going to murder him.'

'Very good, sir.'

Elsewhere I have described a scene I once witnessed on a Channel steamer. I would not be prepared to swear in a witness box that it all happened exactly as here related, but my description is, nevertheless, pretty near the truth. Only another man and myself were on deck and a violent storm was raging. A tremendous gale was lashing mountainous seas. We huddled there for a while, without uttering one single word. Suddenly a fearful gust blew the other chap overboard. His head emerged just once from the water below me. He looked at me calmly and remarked somewhat casually:

'Rather windy, isn't it?'

Understatement is not simply a manner of making jokes; in England it is also a way of life. Other people use understatement too – the English do not own the copyright. A cartoon in the *New Yorker* showed two men on the flying trapeze and one has just missed the other's hand, ninety feet up in the air. The man who made the somewhat absent-minded mistake said: 'Ooop, sorry.' Surely, an understatement and an American understatement at that. But in other countries understatement is casual, incidental; in England it flows from the national character; it is in the air.

It is, more often than not, not even meant as a joke. When an Englishman leaves his house in pouring rain and meets his suburban neighbour on the way to the underground station, he will remark: 'It's not so nice, is it?' When someone expands a theory at the club bar or in the drawing-room and sounds firm and opinionated – rather un-English – someone else will remark: 'You really think so?' In a more temperamental Continental country, the reaction would sound something like this: 'You are talking utter rot, and it is beneath my dignity to give you a proper answer.' If someone tells an unlikely story, an Englishman will remark at the end – in an admiring tone, perhaps: 'Oh, is that so?' In Italian this would run: 'What you said is a bloody lie and I do not believe one word of it.' 'I am not so sure I like that' – is strong condemnation in this country.

A few days ago I went to see a house warmly recommended by an estate agent who said that if I invested some money in it, I could turn it into a charming little place. I found a filthy street, in vile surroundings, while the house itself should have been described as a ramshackle hut in a state of collapse, unfit for human habitation, to be pulled down, the quicker the better. I looked again at the specification and read: 'In need of modernization.' My anger evaporated instantaneously. It was all my own fault. Having spent thirty-one years in this country, I should have known that 'In need of modernization' means in the language of English estate agents.

Understatement springs from the English character; and having become second nature, it also contributes now to the formation or development of the English character. As I said, it is not only a joke, not always a joke and, occasionally, it is very much the opposite of a joke.

The whole rhythm of life in England is an understatement; their suppression of emotion is an understatement; the under-reaction to everything, the polite word instead of a rude outburst (when the latter would help so much more to clear the air); the stiff upper lip; the very climate with its absence of extremes, all these are understatements. Neville Chamberlain's policy, which contributed considerably to the perils of war and which was incarnated in the notorious phrase about Czechoslovakia being a faraway country about which we knew little, was also an understatement. The Second World War was due mainly to Nazi paranoia; but partly also to the English sense of humour.

Why minor?

At this point it might be useful to halt for a while to consider the question whether the joke is an art form and if it is, why is it a minor art?

The Oxford English Dictionary defines a joke as a thing said or done to excite laughter; witticism, jest; ridiculous circumstance. Nuttall's says: a jest to raise laughs; something witty or sportive; something not serious or in earnest.

One could argue that these definitions are not perfect. But as (a) everybody can argue that *no* definition is perfect, and (b) we all know what a joke is – I shall not waste too many words on this point.

It is obvious that inventing a joke is a creative activity which should come under the definition of art. Telling a joke is a *performance*; it is performing art.

Having accepted this, we are inclined both to under-estimate and to over-estimate the art of inventing and telling jokes. The first derogatory argument is this: 'But everybody can tell a joke.' True; but most people do it badly or just tolerably. Everybody can sing, too, yet singing remains an art; everybody can draw *somehow*, yet Picassos are rare. Society is also inclined to go to the other extreme and to over-estimate jokes. Society expresses its appreciation mostly in cash and it certainly overpays its jesters. I am not speaking now of serious comic artists, comedy-writers, humorists, who belong to another category; I am speaking of the compere type of chap of stage and television, who tells us quick-firing jokes, and his ally and supplier, the gag-man – and as I mentioned at the beginning of the book – humorists turn gag-men for the rewards and forget how to write in the process.

Jokes, in addition to making us laugh – if they do – have quite a lot of other useful roles in life. The chap who buttonholes you in the Club, asks you if you have heard the latest and then proceeds to pour out endless stories – is, of course, the proverbial arch-bore. People who spend busy evenings just telling one another jokes, are even worse. They, in addition to being bores, express the neurosis and brainlessness of an increasing number of people who carry on canned conversation. Ready-made jokes enable them to shine and feel gloriously witty, without contributing one single observation or remark of their own.

The question for us is this: what can possibly raise jokes to a higher level? By what warrant may the joke be called one of the arts? When is a joke something more than a mere raiser of laughs?

First of all, a joke can put things, definitions, ideas in a nutshell.

Green meets his friend, Brown, who asks him how he is.

'Terrible. Desperate,' replies Green, and goes on to tell Brown that he wets the bed – a nasty habit he cannot get rid of, and which is ruining his marriage, his extra-marital sex-life and his nerves.

'But why don't you go to a psychoanalyst?' Brown asks him. Green is rather reluctant but Brown talks him into it.

Six months later they meet again and a glance at Green is enough to show that now he is a happy man.

'So you went to the psychoanalyst?' says Brown.

'Yes, I did.'

'Did he help you?'

'Very much so'.

'You don't wet the bed any more, then?'

'Yes, I still do. But now I am proud of it.'

Few long essays could explain the effects of psychoanalytical treatment better than this joke.

Secondly, jokes can elucidate things, often more revealingly than long and complicated scientific definitions. When I was a law-student in Budapest, I had a Professor – one of the country's great jurists – who had the habit of clarifying points with the help of jokes. I still remember not only the jokes, but also the legal points they demonstrated, while I have forgotten many other more important – but duller – matters.

For example, the possible defences open to a respondent are important from the point of view of burden of proof. In certain cases the respondent had to prove his own statement; in other cases, the nature of the defence transferred this burden to the plaintiff.

You simply deny the plaintiff's statement, for example. He says he has lent you a hundred pounds and you say he has not. He has to prove that, in fact, you owe him this sum. Or the respondent pleads ignorance. The plaintiff may or may not have lent him the money, he does not remember. In this case, again, the plaintiff has to prove that, in fact, he has lent the money. What can be duller, the reader may ask, than all this? We came then to the dullest defence of all, what Hungarian law called an excuse.

'*The excuse*,' my Professor went on, 'is a defence in which the respondent accepts the plaintiff's case, but alleges some other facts which make the plaintiff's case invalid. If someone pleads an excuse, he must accept the burden of proof with it. Do you understand this?'

We said we did, but we did not. Then he told us a story which enlightened the problem with unparalleled clarity. His stories nearly always came from a corner of Hungary where legal morality was not supposed to be too high and perjured witnesses were simply a matter of price.

Green goes to the lawyer and tells him that Brown has sued him for a hundred pounds (let us forget about local currency). The lawyer asks him if he really owes Brown the money but Green is most emphatic and obviously sincere in hotly denying it.

'Very well,' says the lawyer, 'then we'll go to court and deny Brown's allegations.'

Green shakes his head:

'We are doing nothing of the sort. We go to court, admit that Brown lent me the money, but we state that I have paid him back.'

The lawyer is astonished.

'Why complicate things? What's the use of doing that?'

'Because in this case,' replies Green, 'it's me that's bringing the two false witnesses.'

I think even to the dullest student it became quite clear what burden of proof meant in the case of an *excuse*.

The same Professor explained the multiple defence – and its occasionally questionable value – with this example:

In the old days in Iran, that famous character, Nasredin, was sued by his neighbour who alleged that Nasredin had borrowed a beautiful, brand new jug from him and returned it chipped and broken. Nasredin offered a threefold defence: He said that (a) he had never borrowed the jug from his neighbour; (b) that it was in immaculate condition when he returned it, and (c) that it was already broken when he got it.

A joke or anecdote can prick pomposity and show up cant and hypocrisy better than any other method. The following is a true story. In one of the Hungarian theatres before the war, there was an extremely able, but utterly unreliable young actor. He was a great artist but an equally great drinker and after his frequent late night bouts he was apt to turn up late for rehearsal. He had been admonished; fined; threatened with dismissal; all to no avail.

One morning he turned up at 11.30 instead of 10 o'clock. He was gloomy and mournful and told the director that his grandmother had died. He shed two or three tears and seemed to be moved. The death of the same grandmother had been used on several previous occasions – this was about the third time she had died – but the director was eager to accept any excuse, avoid another scene and more fuss and get on with the rehearsal. The actor, however, had to keep up appearances and remained mournful as if hard put to control his grief.

By lunchtime everyone was more relaxed and the director asked the actor to join him for lunch.

'Oh, no . . .' he shook his head firmly, 'I can't possibly eat a bite in my great sorrow.'

'You must not give in,' said the director. 'You must think of your children.'

'Ah, well . . .' the actor sighed, went over to the restaurant, ordered a huge steak with fried onions, and ate it all up with tremendous gusto. The director could not resist commenting upon this:

'I am so glad to see,' he said with well-disguised malice, 'that you've managed to overcome your grief.'

The actor looked at his empty plate, sighed again and replied in lugubrious tones:

'This was her favourite dish.'

Or another story – this one about Fritz Kreisler, the great violinist, who lived in New York, putting some snobs in their place. Kreisler's agent was rung up by a new millionaire's wife who wanted Kreisler to play to her guests after dinner. The agent said that he would have to consult Kreisler which he did and phoned back to say that, yes, the artist was willing to play for ten thousand dollars. The lady nearly fainted; that was a tremendous amount of money just for two short pieces; it was an indecent sum to ask, even if the audience did consist of the richest businessmen in New York, etc., etc. She was so persistent that the agent agreed to consult Kreisler again, but came back to say that ten thousand dollars was Kreisler's price and they could take it or leave it. They took it. When, on the day of the party, Kreisler came along after dinner, the master of the house, the *nouveau riche* manufacturer, drew him aside and told him that he wanted to make it quite clear that after the performance Mr Kreisler would not be required to stay to mingle with the guests.

Kreisler replied:

'Had I known that I was not expected to mingle with the guests, I would have come for three thousand.'

Jokes without an *a propos* can be an awful bore; but a joke told as a parallel, a parable – can cut really deep. There was a funny weekly in Budapest which had a permanent feature: a man goes to ask advice of the Wise Old Rabbi who always replies with a story – seemingly unconnected with the questions, but, in fact, most revealing. Here's an example:

'Tell me, Rabbi,' the question goes, 'how is it with those strikers? They always choose the most awkward moment to strike and yet they always tell us how terribly sorry they are for the public. Are they happy or sad?'

The Rabbi thinks this over and tells the man:

'Cohen's wife dies and before the funeral he is told that he would have to ride to the cemetery in the same car as his mother-in-law.'

'Why should I?' he asks

'This was your wife's last wish.'

'Well, if I must – I must. But I tell you, this will spoil my day.'

Or a Jew might go to the Rabbi and ask him:

'Tell me, how is it that the British invade Anguilla with helicopters, marines and paratroops – the whole lot – and then they recognize the existing government? If they recognize them, why was it necessary to go and invade?'

The Rabbi says:

'Cohen's wife – when there are some guests in the house – shouts at him and orders him to get under the table. Cohen crawls under the table. A few minutes later, Mrs Cohen tells him:

'Come out!'

Cohen stays under the table.

Mrs Cohen shouts at him:

'I told you to come out.'

Cohen replies:

'No. I'll stay where I am. That will show you who is master of this house.'

*　　*　　*

Or what can be more devastating than a parable – a true story, by the way – I heard in Israel, soon after the Six Day War?

After the first – the 1948 – Arab–Jewish war, most of the great Palestinian *seigneurs* fled from Israel and this, for the first time in history, gave a chance to humbler men to become mayors and other leaders of the community. The departed members of the great, feudal families settled in Jordan, where many of them were caught after the June War and found themselves under Israeli occupation. The feudal gentlemen looked down upon the upstarts who came to visit them now: they may have had all the virtues, but they lacked birth and birth was the only real virtue these *seigneurs* appreciated.

Soon after the Six Day War the new, self-made mayor of an Israeli Arab township went to visit its one-time feudal mayor on the West Bank of the Jordan, now in Israeli-occupied territory. The new mayor expected to be embraced by the old man but in fact he was received coolly and with condescension. There were about a dozen people in the old mayor's house, his friends and relations. Coffee and cold drinks were served in Arab fashion. Then the old man told a parable.

'There was an Alsatian dog who wanted to become a wolf. So he went to an old wolf and told him about his desire.'

'It's all very well to want to become a wolf,' the old wolf told the dog, 'and I know you *look* like a wolf. But if you want to *be* a wolf, you must behave like a wolf, not like a dog.'

'How do wolves behave?'

'The number one rule is that when wolves meet, they smell one another's noses and not one another's behinds.'

The dog thanked the old wolf, went to live with the wolves and behaved as they did. Nineteen years later (that was the time that passed between the '48 War and the Six Day War) the dog and the old wolf met again. The dog went up to him and started smelling his nose, wolf-like. But the old wolf told him:

'I know you are only a dog. You might as well smell my behind.'

The Israeli Arab visitor jumped up, and walked 'out of the room, never to return. I am not unaware of the nastiness of this story; but as a devastating, vicious, personal attack it is hard to beat.

Or take the political joke – another case where the joke, while it must be funny in its own right, has a deeper, more significant meaning. I shall have a great deal more to say about political jokes; for the present I simply give one example from the late fifties. Many long essays were written – both by eastern and western economists – on the subject of

Hungary's economic plight and the deflation of the currency and I read quite a few of them. But none explained the position as clearly – let alone as briefly – as this story, emanating, by the way, from Budapest.

A Hungarian communist official was sent to Paris on state business. As soon as he arrived, he visited a brothel. (There are no brothels in Paris but Hungarians then had not yet heard of their abolition.) Madame received him and the man chose a girl, Giselle, and took her upstairs. A few minutes later, Giselle came down shouting excitedly: 'No . . . not that! There is a limit to everything!'

Madame frowned and sent up Mimi, a much more hardened professional. But Mimi, too, came dashing down a few minutes afterwards, very indignant and with tears in her eyes.

'No . . . certainly not *that*! How disgusting!'

Well, Madame decides she had better see for herself but, to be sure, she too leaves the room with the utmost indignation, shouting 'Certainly not that!' and 'There is a limit to everything.'

An old client of the house who had witnessed the whole scene asks Madame what it is the man wanted. Madame replies, still seething with indignation:

'He wants to pay with Hungarian money.'

Jokes like these, when they clarify a point, illustrate an idea, serve as parables to deflate pride, demolish snobbishness, and pomposity, all belong to the sphere of minor art.

But why *minor*? – you might be inclined to ask.

To be a minor art – to be ranked with ballroom dancing, or television interviewing – is no degradation. But there are three good reasons why they are and *must* remain minor art.

1 Humour and comedy must unavoidably always remain a minor art. This does not mean that any 'serious' writer, any humourless dullard, is superior to the great humorous artists. It takes quite a writer to be superior to, say, Mark Twain. But if you take Shakespeare himself, his greatest tragedy *is* superior to his best comedy. *King Lear* is a greater piece of art than *The Merchant of Venice*; the *Taming of the Shrew* cannot hold a candle to *Macbeth*. (This thesis has been questioned, but I hold to it.) The main reason for this, I feel, is that tragedy goes the whole hog, delves into the depths of the human soul and faces the consequences, while comedy evades, explodes, deflates, absolves tension in punch-lines and – in fact – runs away from reality. As I have said, there is something cowardly in humour.

But there is also something infinitely wise. A coward is, as a rule, wiser than a reckless, undaunted hero.

2 The joke is one-dimensional. It cannot aspire to be a true mirror of the human situation – which is always complicated and multifarious. The Wise Old Rabbi may be quite a good Rabbi, a pious and learned leader, a man of warm heart and a flaming tongue, a great preacher and scholar, but every time we meet him, he's telling us comic parables; the commercial traveller of the jokes may be an excellent salesman, a good father and gentle husband, an efficient golfer and stamp-collector, but we always meet him as a funny man, delivering the punch-lines to jokes; and those two famous Jews may also be great characters – people worth knowing – but we never really meet them; they're always sitting in the proverbial railway-carriage, their dialogue is pungent, short and one-dimensional.

3 This brevity is the final reason for the low artistic status of the joke. Any proper form of art must have some length because there may be beauty in short pieces, like Chinese and Japanese poems, but, without length, there is no development, there is no construction.

Molnar, the playwright, was right when he discussed this problem with his friend, Alfred Polgar. Polgar was a Viennese writer of aphorisms, paradoxes, wise sayings. He was witty and attractive, but his pieces consisted of a few unconnected sentences and sayings. Molnar encouraged him to write something longer, more substantial: something that had to be built up, that needed construction. But Polgar – a modest man – shook his head and insisted that that particular form suited his talent best. Molnar gave up and shrugged his shoulders:

'Very well, then. You will remain the world champion of the one-yard sprint.'

That is the difficulty with the joke as an art form. It is sad that *quantity* should rear its ugly head even when we are discussing art, however minor. Yet, the truth remains that even the best joke necessarily remains the one-yard sprint.

Folk art

Understatement, as an atmosphere, an ambiance, a way of life, is unique to England. But the love of self-mockery, self-criticism, occasionally even self-derision, the English – perhaps I can speak here of the British – share with the Jews. English and Jewish humour share this one characteristic – this ability to laugh at themselves, but differ in everything else.

I have written humorous and satirical books on quite a number of peoples, which were received in England and in Israel quite differently from the way they were received elsewhere.

I have mentioned that having been outspoken and critical about peoples – I expected storms to break over me – storms which never came. Sometimes I wonder if I really *wanted* those storms; or was I, in fact, pleased that they blew over before they broke out? – and that people, instead of trying to assassinate me, patted me on the back and said: 'Quite amusing!' But – whatever psychologists may say, not *all* so-called niceness is just disguised nastiness. I criticized people, described people in a funny way (because I saw them in a funny light) and made fun of them. But never, for a moment, did I sit in judgment over them and I hated it when critics – more often abroad than in Britain – described me as one castigating vice, unmasking hypocrisy and standing up for true virtue. It always upset me to see myself portrayed in such a pompous role. Who am I to tell people where to get off? Who am I 'to castigate'? All I tried to do was to describe people as I saw them. But as I see it, in all my writings, one foolish and erratic man makes fun of other foolish and erratic men – it is never a case of the just and wise man showing the straight and narrow path to lesser mortals. Whenever I read a phrase like 'Mr M. does not suffer fools gladly' – I blush. I *do* suffer fools gladly. I am one of them. We all are. Humanity cannot be divided into fools and non-fools. All of us belong to both categories. The most brilliant among us are hopeless fools in many respects; while the most hopeless asses easily surpass their brilliant fellows in certain situations. A man – intellectually a giant – may be emotionally a child, or worse: an adolescent; and indeed the great Freud himself – who threw a great deal of light on the human psyche and changed humanity's view of itself – could be as childish and petty in certain cases as other silly mortals.

People's reactions to my various books were interesting. Many people – the French, for example – did not care. If they read my book at all, they put it aside, sometimes with a good-natured smile, sometimes without it. Certain countries disliked what I had written but they knew that 'one had to take it'; they knew it was foolish to protest. They realized that a humorist had set a trap and that nothing was to be gained by howling at him; if he is right, he is right; if he is wrong, he can always plead: 'I was only joking'. The Swiss – a rather ponderous and humourless people on the whole – protested loudly; 'we have a wonderful sense of humour', they claimed and then the head of a Swiss tourist organization – having protested loudest of all – suppressed a rather innocently funny film I had made about the Swiss, thus squandering the large amount of public money he had spent on it – an even more unnatural thing for a Swiss to do than laughing at himself. But he could not see or take a joke about the Swiss.

Storms, as I have complained before, I caused but rarely. One Italian gentleman wrote me a letter after the publication of my *Italy for Beginners*, saying that while he had not read it, he had been informed that I was libelling his country and would I name the date, the time, and the place when and where I would meet him for a duel, and would I also choose the weapons. I answered that I would meet him at 7 a.m. on an autumn day in St James's Park, outside Buckingham Palace, with heavy cavalry sabres; but at the same time I advised him also to read my book. A fortnight later I received another letter from my would-be opponent who said that he had now read my book, found it complimentary to the great Italian nation, and he would be grateful if I would allow him to call me his friend for the rest of his life. I allowed him to do so.

Another storm – just a shade more serious – broke out in Liechtenstein

– after the publication of an affectionate and flattering portrait in *Encounter* (or rather the republication of the piece in various German and Swiss newspapers). The national newspaper of Liechtenstein (a publication appearing twice weekly) delivered a thunderous attack on me and I was happy and felt important. A few years later, however, Princess Gina, the wife of the ruling Prince, Franz Joseph, referred to my book in an interview with Swiss television, saying that she liked it very much. I was genuinely pleased by these generous remarks but, of course, it completely destroyed the value of the Liechtenstein press attack.

I was assured that if there was any nation in the world which ferociously resented criticism, it was the Australians. This was absolutely true ten years before and while there are quite a lot of thick-headed reactionaries about there even today who take any critical remark as 'knocking', most people received my book kindly and said it was 'fair enough'. The one reviewer who made a hysterical attack on me – in a rather primitive 'who the hell does this guy think he is to criticize the finest country in the world' style – was an immigrant.

Perhaps it was the American who most strongly resented a non-American daring to criticize God's Own Country but that was two decades ago. The climate of opinion has changed there, too, and in fact they are in a rather self-derogatory mood nowadays.

There are, however, two countries which did not mind in the least if I was rude about them (which, I hope, I never was): the English and the Israelis. They loved my jokes at their expense and proceeded to offer me more and better ones against themselves. Both the English and the Jews invented these jokes against themselves before others invented them. Yet, how different their laughter! How utterly different, in content and in context!

The Jews *needed* the jokes, the English did not.

Jewish humour was born in the Empire of the Czars where the Jews were persecuted, kicked around, looked down upon, yet remained convinced – with reason – that they were no worse, not less valuable human beings, than their coarse, uneducated and corrupt oppressors. Their only means of saving their self-respect, indeed of surviving, was to laugh at their tormentors. Many of these jokes are about anti-semitism on the one hand and about superior Jewish cleverness on the other.

A Czarist officer is travelling in a train when, to his disgust, an Orthodox Jew, with side whiskers and wearing a *kaftan* – gets in and sits down opposite him. To his greater disgust, the Jew produces a bag with a lot of smelly herrings and starts eating. After some time, the officer speaks:

'I say, Jew,' he says, 'you are supposed to be clever. Will you give me your secret? *What* makes you so damn clever?'

'It's very simple, Lieutenant: it's the herring heads.'

'What the hell do you mean?' asks the officer.

'Just what I say. We eat herring heads and that makes us clever. Why don't you try? I have here herring heads and I am quite prepared to sell you a few – twenty kopecks each cash.'

'But herring heads?' says the officer. 'It's disgusting.'

'You don't *have* to eat it . . .' says the Jew. 'But if you want to be clever . . .'

'All right . . . give me three.'

The officer pays the sixty kopecks and he eats the first head with utter disgust, then the other two with increased nausea. Having eaten all three, he tells the Jew:

'I say, Jew . . . what a swindler you are. . . . A *whole* of these herrings costs five kopecks and you have sold me their heads for twenty each.'

The Jew looks at him approvingly and says:

'You see: already it works!'

Such jokes were invented by Jews and told by Jews against themselves. The joke just told shows the Jew as a bit of a clever cheat – but nothing really bad. But there are more ferocious jokes – all invented by Jews – which have an almost anti-semitic edge. Jews are fully aware of this, but they explain: 'The joke can't be anti-semitic, if *we* are telling it.' But it can, of course; there *is* such a thing as unconscious self-hatred and the Jewish anti-semite is no rarity. These jokes seem to have an unattractive element: there is nothing more destructive than accepting yourself at your enemies' valuation.

To accept yourself at your enemies' valuation is an extreme case and it is certain that not all those who invent and repeat Jewish jokes go as far as that. It seems obvious that without accepting anything the anti-semites say and think, the Jewish joke has a strong masochistic element. That does not really detract from its attractive qualities: masochists are, on the whole, nicer people than sadists. (I am not speaking, of course, of masochistic perverts. But all of us belong to either of two classes of people; we are either sadistically or masochistically inclined.

And the masochistically inclined people are those who, in common parlance, would be described as likeable, tolerant, often sweet.)

These jokes have been explained in various ways and they serve various psychological needs – in addition to the political ones already mentioned.

Humour always comforts you; to some extent it helps to extricate you from a sad, even unbearable situation. Self-irony is also self-consolation; it cheers you up. But self-irony is also a preventive mechanism: it wards off an anticipated attack. This self-irony, even occasional self-degradation, is not capitulation to your enemies: it does not have to mean accepting yourself at their valuation. On the contrary, it may contain a great deal of defiance. It may signify: you don't need to decry and attack us, we see ourselves more clearly and we do it ourselves. Indeed, in many cases, this defiance goes even further: *you* want to paint our picture, *you* want to disparage and malign us, poor fools? Even *that* we do much better than you in our own jokes about ourselves.

Defiance never exists without an element of true pride. The most self-derogatory story has as much pride in it as it has humility. It implies self-criticism, no doubt; but it also means – that's what I am, that's what I remain; and – if I can afford so much against myself, I must be a fine fellow indeed.

The masochist longs for love and the self-critical Jewish jokes too contain a strong element of an appeal for love. 'Look at me,' plead these jokes, 'how wretched, poor, defenceless and weak I am. You must love me, you really must.'

Once I heard a very learned and pious non-Jewish gentleman explain that the Bible itself ordered Jews to tell jokes about themselves.

'It's Matthew,' he said. 'And whosoever shall exalt himself, shall be abased; and he that shall humble himself, shall be exalted.'

Perhaps. The Jews have always been a pious people and, maybe, they just have their superb sense of humour because God Almighty advised them to be funny.

But while on the subject of religion, it would, perhaps, be more to the point to compare Jewish jokes with confessions. After all, these jokes are nothing else than an admission of sins, mistakes, weaknesses and faults – just like confessions. Confession purifies, brings relief and cleanses us of our guilt. Is it possible that the Jewish joke is partly a means of gaining absolution?

*   *   *

The Jewish joke is terribly repetitive. It has been suggested that Cain slew Abel because he kept pestering him with long-winded Jewish jokes. These jokes have, on the whole, only a few main themes: the Jew and the Gentile, the Jew and his Rabbi, the Rabbi and the Catholic priest, the eternal fugitive, the rich Jew and the poor Jew, the *schnorrer* (the poor man who tries borrowing from the rich, the undeserving chap who manages to live on charity), the Yiddisher Mama, the baptized Jew and the *schadchen*, the marriage-broker, whose tongue turns ugly women into seductive beauties. ('But she is a hunchback!' an alarmed would-be client exclaims in one of these jokes, seeing the proposed girl's picture. The *schadchen* kisses his fingertips with delight and replies: 'But *what* a hump!')

Almost all critics of Jewish humour admit that these jokes are rarely cynical, and they are hardly ever violent. (A well-known story tells about the Jewish soldier in World War I who shouts at the enemy in the opposite trench: 'Are you *meschugge* to shoot this way? There are *people* here.')

Sterner critics discover a paranoid element in the jokes. Theodor Reik quotes the story of the Jewish nurse. She has spent the night with a very sick patient and when the doctor arrives in the morning, he enquires how his patient is. The nurse replies: 'Oh, he was sick all night, kept calling me . . . he wanted this and that . . . God, what a horrible night I had . . .' This story is supposed to reflect self-centredness and, as I have said, paranoid tendencies. I only see it as the usual, disarming Jewish self-criticism: our nurses care more for themselves than for their charges – but who doesn't?

Far from seeing paranoid tendencies, Dr Grotjahn[6] doubts even the strong masochistic tendencies in Jewish jokes. He writes:

'The Jewish joke, however, is only a masochistic mask; it is by no means a masochistic perversion. The Jewish joke constitutes victory by defeat. The persecuted Jew who makes himself the butt of the joke deflects his dangerous hostility away from the persecutors onto himself. The result is not defeat or surrender but victory and greatness.'

No one has explained more clearly the ambivalent masochistic and sadistic – apologetic and aggressive – tendencies of some of the jokes than Dr Grotjahn. He tells us the joke about the mother who gave two neckties to her son for his birthday. The son, to please his mother, put one of the ties on straight away. The mother asked him reproachfully: 'Don't you like the other one?'

Dr Grotjahn comments: 'What happened here? The aggressive

thought: "Mothers are no good. Mothers are tricky. Mothers turn things around. A son never wins" is repressed, disguised, and then admitted to consciousness. Repressive energy is freed and is released in laughter. The masochistic element becomes visible in the thought: "Mothers want to suffer. They turn things against themselves, no matter how. A son does not need to feel guilty about that." '

An example of the same sadistic-masochistic ambivalence.
A Jewish lady is travelling on a New York bus, sitting near the driver. She asks him:
'Are you Jewish?'
'No,' the driver replies curtly.
They travel two more stages and the lady is obviously not to be put off lightly. She asks again:
'Are you Jewish?'
'I've told you I am not,' says the bus-driver.
Three stops later:
'You *are* Jewish, aren't you?'
The bus-driver sighs and admits it:
'Of course I'm Jewish.'
The lady looks at him carefully and remarks:
'You don't look it.'
First, she aggressively asserts their bond and identity but as soon as the man breaks down and admits the tie, it is denied him.

This tie, this bond, this identity is an essential part of the jokes. Perhaps the seemingly anti-semitic joke is not an admission of 'guilt' at all, not an acceptance of oneself at the anti-semite's valuation but something very different and much healthier. Jokes do create a bond and establish solidarity. Laughter creates comradeship between the Jews who laugh at themselves when no one else overhears them; but laughter creates love and understanding too. Tell the Jewish joke to the anti-semite and if he laughs he will be less anti-semitic. The Jewish joker may – to some extent – present himself in these jokes as the anti-semite wishes to see him; but as soon as he presents himself to the anti-semite in this light, he fights and erodes anti-semitism. Theodor Reik, in his book *Jewish Wit*,[7] writes: '. . . it can only be considered progress that more and more Jewish jokes are appreciated and enjoyed by wide circles of American Gentiles. "Laugh and the world laughs

89

with you" was not always true some decades ago when Jewish jokes were told to a Gentile audience. It is so today.'

Who is right in this argument, after all? Those who see the Jewish jokes as a manifestation of Jewish anti-semitism? Or those who see in them a means of combating anti-semitism? Are they self-degrading or defiant? Are they expressions of humility or pride? Are they mystic confessions of guilt and ways of seeking absolution, or self-assured shouts into the ears of Gentiles: 'That's what we are, that's what we remain.'

Let me quote Theodor Reik again:

'Those fans of our mothers and grandmothers were used for several purposes: they provided refreshing coolness in the heat of the summer and in the ballroom; they were used to flirt with; to demonstrate certain feelings; and, finally, to hide those feelings from the world and oneself. Similarly, Jewish jokes serve various purposes: to bring relaxation in the ardour of battle with the seen and with the invisible enemy; to attract him as well as to repel him; and last, but certainly not least, to conceal onself behind them. Jewish wit hides as much as it discloses.'

And now a look at the other nation who is a great hand at self-mockery. A young English girl is asked:

'Where did you spend your holiday?'

'At Majorca.'

'Where is that?'

'I don't know. We flew.'

This joke pokes fun at the innocence of the English, but it is an innocent joke, a kind one; it does not cut deep, it does not hurt. Among other things, it also reflects the English lack of interest in foreigners and foreign parts. Perhaps it is silly of the girl not to know where she is; but, after all, who cares? One goes to places to enjoy the sun and the sea – but one does not really bother about the precise geographical details. In a way, this joke reflects English superiority over foreigners, just as one of our former jokes reflected Jewish superiority over the Russian officer. But the Jews have to *strive* for this superiority and make an effort to maintain it; to the English it comes naturally; it's inborn. The English do not boast of this superiority – they are much better mannered than to boast of anything. They are almost apologetic about it: it's there, they feel, they cannot help it.

Where did the British gain this self-assurance, this belief in themselves? A nation, just like an individual, is the product of its past and environment and the English have a very different past from the Jews. The Jews were oppressed, the English oppressed others; the Jews were deprived of their country, the English deprived others; the Jews were barely tolerated even in those lands which they had a right to regard as their own homeland; the English tolerated native populations wherever they happened to find them. The Jews were underdogs; the English top dogs.

But because the English travelled all over the world – and settled in most of it – they were used to the curious glances of people who scrutinized them with awe and hatred, admiration and dislike, envy and hostility, sycophancy and defiance. They were interested in looking at themselves through these people's eyes. They found other people's views funny and instinctive. The English are quite prepared to take note of whatever natives and funny foreigners may think of them: but they do not really care.

Both the Jews and the English are able to laugh at themselves. But, for the reasons explained, there is a difference in the laughter. The Jewish jokes are a little self-conscious, apologetic, occasionally, almost anti-semitic and often very unsure of themselves. The English laugh at themselves, because they are interested in themselves, because they want to be discussed and examined. But whatever others may say about them, they know – without the slightest shadow of doubt – *who* the finest people in this world are.

Now let us return from the world of psychology to the world of politics. A joke in England is a joke; a Jewish joke in Eastern and Central Europe is a serious matter. In a free society the joke is like a pleasant spice – just an after-dinner anecdote which goes down well with coffee and brandy. In lands more familiar with oppression, a joke is necessary for one's self-esteem. Laughter is the only weapon the oppressed can use against the oppressor. It is an aggressive weapon and a safety-valve at one and the same time.

Under political tyranny (under Nazi, or Communist, oppression), political jokes (and more about them later) assume an added significance. In England (or other free countries) a joke or a cartoon repeats – more concisely, more pungently – what the critics, the leading articles, parliamentary debates, speakers at public meetings and even demonstrations say in different language. But under a political tyranny these same jokes – whispered into people's ears – replace the critics, the leading articles, the public debates and the demonstrations. Their very brevity is a God-sent gift: they make their point briefly and impressively – they can be told in a few seconds – so the danger of a lengthy tête-à-tête is avoided. The jokes help to undermine the tyrant's authority and cut him down to human level – or to the sub-human level where he often belongs – and reassure both the purveyor and the audience of the joke.

Here the joke assumes a sociological and political significance, denied to many other art forms. The joke is an art of rebellion at its best. It is – even in less dramatic circumstances – a folk art, indeed, the folk song of an urban population.

Lost in transit

The Jewish joke is probably the best of all jokes and if one wonders why and how the Jews survived several thousand years of persecution, and diaspora, one would count among the decisive factors their sense of humour. If you take your oppressors and persecutors seriously – you will, sooner or later, take over their valuation of yourself, you will feel guilty and will see yourself through their eyes. Take the despots seriously and you will be broken by them and you will, eventually, perish. But if you are able to laugh at them – see their stupidity, their vanity and meanness – if you realize the fatuity of their claims to superiority – then oppression will steel you, make you stronger, more united as a group, and victory – or at least liberation – becomes possible. I am sure that the Jews of antiquity, wandering in the desert for forty years, were sustained not only by prayer, by Moses' strength of character and by manna from heaven, but also by Jewish jokes.

New York humour – it is widely acknowledged – is mostly Jewish. Few people would argue about this and there is nothing miraculous in it, considering the large number of Jews in New York. There is probably a substantial element of Irish humour, too, in America, a very different brand from Jewish humour. When I came to England in 1938 I knew the Scots, Welsh and Irish existed, but I knew very little about them, who they were and what they were like. A friend of mine – another Hungarian journalist – had to go over to Dublin and, on his return, I asked him with great interest what sort of people the Irish were.

'It's quite amazing,' he said. 'They are all Hungarians and they all speak English.'

There was some truth in this. The Irish are open-hearted, hospitable, extrovert, pugnacious and pig-headed like the Hungarians. Approach them nicely as a foreign guest and they will take their shirts off their backs and be pleased to give them to you; but rile them or try to order them around and they will become obstinate and hostile. Irish humour is more robust, less sophisticated, less self-mocking than Jewish – and whenever the two mix, as in America, the mixture produces healthy results.

English humour is remote from the Jewish – although not completely unaffected by it. But with its climate of understatement, with the British lack of ebullience, sentimentality and self-pity, it is a different crop. A comparison of English humour (and that means English character) with American would fill another book. One of the most striking differences is between the Yiddisher Mama atmosphere of New York's Jewish world, and the coolness, often chilliness, of English family life. I was first struck by this coolness during the war. I was playing bridge in an English house with a very English family – father, mother and their daughter – the last-named a lady of twenty-five – while the son of the family was just getting ready to leave and join the army – perhaps never to return (he did, as it happened). He put his coat on, said good-bye to his parents and then came to his sister who told him:

'Good luck to you, darling, all the best. You don't mind if I don't get up to kiss you, but I have *such* an exciting hand.'

Years later I visited another family in the country. I used to know Mary and Basil, but Basil was dead now and I travelled down for the weekend with their daughter and her husband. I knew that Mary and Basil had lived a cat-and-dog life and that the marriage had been near breaking point several times. In fact, I knew that Mary was not inconsolably unhappy when her husband departed for a better world.

But, as I mentioned Basil's name once or twice, the daughter suddenly decided that we ought to go and see her father's grave. Mary was decidedly cool, but the daughter insisted, it was a lovely day, we wanted to take a walk and we might as well walk to the churchyard – about fifteen minutes away. So we went.

The grave was an absolute mess – uncared for, dilapidated and overgrown with weeds. It looked so awful that even Mary seemed to be embarrassed for a moment. Then she said:

'Well, Basil never did like gardening . . .'

I have always cherished this remark – it was as English as they come. It reflected the freezing atmosphere of English family life; it was pragmatic; it was typical English logic, by which I mean that it lacked even the semblance of logic – yet it was funny, it had charm, it was self-mocking and completely disarming.

Central European humour is nothing else, either, than Jewish humour adapted to local circumstances. *Hungarian* humour is feeble – peasant humour; the good *Budapest* jokes, in contrast with Hungarian humour, reflect the Jewish spirit, just as Hungarian middle-class mentality reflects a great deal of Jewish spirit – whether they like it or not. It is natural that this should be so. For a few decades before the First World War, Hungary was wide open to Jewish immigration. Jews were welcome and they flocked into that land of liberalism in large numbers. The Hungarian government – Premier Kalman Tisza, father of the more famous Count Istvan Tisza, premier at the outbreak of the First World War – spoke of this dream of 'twenty million Hungarians' and Jews were encouraged to get Magyarized. This they did; they became more Magyar than the Magyars, they often looked ridiculous and – in true Jewish spirit – they were the first to laugh at themselves. There was no significant Zionist movement in Hungary; Hungarian Jews – even after the awakening following Horthy's White Terror – refused to be Jews; they wanted to be Magyars. Hungary lacked a middle class: the Hungarian aristocracy despised all things Hungarian, the gentry believed that only soldiering, politics and farming were occupations fit for gentlemen. So commerce and banking were left to the Jews and Germans and as a result the Hungarian middle class is a mixture of the German and Jewish spirit – in culture, outlook and humour. Luckily for Budapest, its humour is more Jewish than German. In Vienna, the sociological development was different – the Austrians used to have more of a middle class than the Hungarians – but the result was the same: Viennese humour is essentially Jewish humour – with a Central European accent.
A by-product of all this is the Budapest joke – which used to be good and funny enough. Whatever happened in Hungary – and quite a lot happened, disaster piled upon disaster, lost wars, collapse of regimes, foreign occupation troops, various tyrannies, revolutions, followed by new waves of oppression – Budapest's answer was a joke. The city's reputation as the capital of jokes grew and grew until it became a posture and an attitude. Now Budapest believes that whatever happens – whether in Hungary itself, or Czechoslovakia, or even in the Middle East – the world turns to Budapest expecting its comment in jokes.

They feel they *must* produce *the* joke. They believe that a breathless world does not wait for the American president or Brezhnev to speak; that it does not wait for the reaction of the world press or NATO's next move, but what the jesters of Budapest are going to say. And when you meet a Hungarian after a world event, he will ask you: 'Have you heard the latest?' They are slowly becoming the club-bores of the world. The jokes are sometimes good, but too often they are a rehash of old chestnuts, and the Budapest joke nowadays too often looks a bit faded and pale, like everything else that becomes smug, self-conscious and oracular.

Jewish humour – or rather Jewish jokes – still reign supreme, except in one country: Israel.

That excellent Jewish sense of humour got more or less lost in transit and this is not altogether a loss as far as a nation is concerned. The Jewish sense of humour was the greatest gift against ruthless, brutal oppression – but the Jews of Israel are no longer oppressed. They are a new nation, a pioneering nation, burning with a new nationalism – and the old Jewish sense of humour is being replaced by the sense of humour of a new, developing nation – the sense of humour of, say, Ghana or Upper Volta. From the point of view of world humour, this is not a happy development. It surely adds to the 'humour crisis' and hastens the demise of humour.

Other, more aggressive and sterner qualities are needed in Israel today than the mild self-mockery of the Polish-Jewish jokes. There is no peace in that region, Israel is being forced to become a military camp and the danger exists – many people fear it – that Israel will be forced to become the Prussia of the Middle East. If Jewish humour becomes Prussian humour, that will indeed mean not only the death of humour, but also one of the most grotesque – even frightening – grimaces history has ever made. The day that happens will be the day of the last smile for many of us. But that day seems to be far away. I heard this story – in Israel – about the Six Day War.

A middle-aged gentleman in his fifties went to a Colonel on the first day of the war and said that he, too, wanted to do something for his country. He was told that he was too old but he went on pestering the Colonel who in the end told him:

'Very well. Take these 5,000 leaflets, go up to the Arab lines just in front of us, get rid of the leaflets and come back as soon as you can.'

The man returned four days later and asked for another job. The Colonel shook his head:

'I told you you are no good. What the hell were you doing for four full days?'

The man is a little indignant.

'But, excuse me, Colonel, it takes time to sell 5,000 leaflets to Arabs.'

This is, of course, the old-style Polish-Jewish joke, about the cunning and slyness of the Jew who is slightly crooked but much more intelligent than his adversary. It seems that the old-fashioned Jewish joke – miraculously – finds its way even into Israel.

Things seem to have come full circle. I have told the next story in another book, but I have to repeat it here.

An Israeli couple are touring Europe with their eleven-year-old boy. In Italy, the child asks his parents:

'Are these people Jews?'

'No, my boy,' his father told him, 'they are Christians.'

In Germany he asks again:

'Are *these* people Jews?'

He is told in Germany, in Holland and in Sweden: 'No, these people are not Jews, they are Christians.'

Upon which he exclaims with genuine sympathy:

'Poor Christians . . . it must be awful for them to be scattered like that all over the world.'

Political jokes

Under oppressive regimes jokes replace the press, public debates, parliament – and even private discussion – but they are better than any of these. They are better because a serious debate admits two sides, two views; a serious debate puts arguments, which might be considered, turned round, rejected. The joke is a flash of lightning, a thrust with a rapier. It does not put forward the 'argument' that the tyrant is possibly mistaken: it makes a fool of him, pricks his pomposity, brings him down to a human level and proves that he is weak and will one day come crashing down. Every joke told weakens the tyrant, every laugh at his expense is a nail in his coffin. That is why tyrants and their henchmen cannot possibly have a sense of humour, any more than an archbishop can be an atheist or a monarch a republican. No one living in the free atmosphere of a western democracy can imagine the liberating and invigorating effect these jokes have as they spread from mouth to mouth.

In this country it was stated under George III and reaffirmed under the present Master of the Rolls: 'The poorest man may in his cottage bid defiance to all the forces of the Crown. The storm may enter, the rain may enter, but the King of England may not enter. All his forces dare not cross the threshold of the ruined tenement.' The political joke whispered in a land of oppression is certainly Hobbes's 'sudden glory'. In Hitler's or in Stalin's Europe, there were few gleams of light: the intermittent flashes of jokes were among the most reassuring. A joke told in a totalitarian dictatorship is an act of resistance and is most certainly regarded as such by the political police. Many people spent years in prison for telling and indeed for listening to jokes and a few even died for the sake of a good story.

Western jokes may be revealing and even hard-hitting. Here are some examples, one each from France, the United States and Britain. The de Gaulles are waiting for the result of a plebiscite. The General is shaving and the first results are handed over by a messenger to his wife. Madame de Gaulle looks at the report, rushes into the bathroom and says to her husband:

'Mon Dieu, mon Dieu, we are winning!'

'I have already told you, Yvonne,' the General tells her coolly, 'that when no one else is present, you can call me Charles.'

Before the 1968 presidential elections in America, there was only very limited enthusiasm for either candidate. People were fond of telling one another:

'Cheer up! Only one of them can be elected.'

Or take one of the Balogh-Kaldor jokes from Britain: Members of Parliament were complaining that one of the first Finance Bills was terribly complicated, practically incomprehensible. Someone retorted:

'That's nothing. You should have read it in the original Hungarian.'

Laughter is sometimes called (in a different context) the luxury reflex. In the west it is indeed a luxury. Jokes are not necessities. They are only one out of many possible ways of criticism. In totalitarian countries jokes are the *only* way. The next step after the joke is the political assassination or rebellion. There is nothing in between.

It would be possible to write the history of the twentieth century based on jokes. I remember how impressed I was when reading, as a young man in Hungary, André Maurois's *Disraeli* and finding that whenever he wanted to explain a political situation or crisis, he always described the contemporary *Punch* cartoon about it, which was, as a rule, more enlightening than the political speeches. Yes, it would be possible to tell the history of the last few decades in jokes, but it would also be monotonous and tiresome. So I shall not attempt it. But I shall draw a quick portrait of two eras, just to show how these political jokes work. In the thirties, frightened – and now we know how justly frightened – Jews from Germany and Central Europe were trying to get visas into *any* country prepared to let them in. These charitable countries were few and far between. On the whole, the happier and more attractive lands did not want to let Jews in because they did not want to annoy the Nazis; besides, there was an economic crisis everywhere and fresh arrivals looking for work were not welcome. The few countries which were opening their doors a little wider than most, were not the most attractive on earth. Someone anxious to save his skin – one might imagine – would not be too choosy *who* saves his skin. But human nature being what it is, he *is*. It was in these days that this sad joke was popular:

A Jew goes to the British Consulate where he is told that Britain, unfortunately, is out for him, but he is given friendly advice.

'Why don't you go to Morocco?'

'Oh, it's too hot,' the Jew replies.

'The Philippines?'

'Too tropical.'

'Bolivia?'

'There's yellow fever there.'

'Venezuela?'

'Malaria.'

'Iceland?'

'Too cold.'

'Shanghai?'

'You can't make a living there.'

'United States?'

'I am not wanted there.'

'Well,' says the Consul a little impatiently, 'have a look at the globe and tell me where you want to go.'

The Jew looks at the globe, turns it round and round for a long time and in the end, asks the Consul:

'Haven't you got another globe?'

For a short while after the Nazis came to power, they respected public opinion in other lands and were reluctant to antagonize it.

An old, orthodox Jew walks along the Kurfürstendamm in Berlin – in long, black robe, side-whiskers, little skull-cap and all. Two beefy S.A. men eye him, and then approach him menacingly. The old Jew asks them:

'What's the matter? Haven't you ever seen a Swiss citizen before?'

Another story from the same period:

An old Jew stops at the statue of General Moltke where a young Prussian officer is already standing. The old Jew asks the Prussian – with a strong Yiddish accent:

'Excuse me, Lieutenant, is this General Moltke?'
The officer replies, ironically imitating the man's ugly accent.
'Yes . . . this is General Moltke.'
The old Jew asks him, reproachfully:
'Why do you imitate *me*? Imitate *him*.'
To follow through the Nazi era would be too distressing, so let us turn to the Communists.

The Russians occupied Central Europe and while they often behaved in a most uncivilized manner – their crimes ranged from stealing watches to raping women – one was not supposed to speak of these matters; one had to speak of the glorious Red Army only in terms of gratitude. In those days – when even clothing was in very short supply, one nasty but fashionable crime was to force people to undress in the street, even in mid-winter, and make off with all their clothes.

Mr C., a citizen of Budapest – is found stark naked in the street. A Hungarian policeman is about to arrest him, when Mr C. explains that he has been attacked and forced to undress by a man who got away with all his clothes.
'What sort of man?' asks the policeman.
'I have no idea.'
'How was he dressed?'
'In a khaki uniform, flat peaked cap, epaulettes, belt, and long boots.'
'Well, that was a Russian soldier.'
Mr C. holds up his hand:
' *You* said it, not me.'

In the days when Stalin was deciding on all scientific matters, and the geneticist Lysenko was his blue-eyed boy, while at the same time, the Russians were busy robbing satellite countries, it was said in Budapest that Professor Lysenko had developed a new animal, a cross between the giraffe and the cow.
'And what can it do?'
'His neck is long enough to feed in Hungary, but it is milked in Russia.'
Next there came a period when the newspapers were full of boasts about miraculous technical advances, while people were, in fact, plagued by ridiculous shortages of everyday articles.
'If things go on like this,' said Kovacs, 'I'll soon have a helicopter.'
'A helicopter? What do you need a helicopter for?'

'Suppose we hear that one can buy shoe-laces near Lake Balaton. Then I jump into my helicopter and fly there to get a pair of shoe-laces.'

As freedom was disappearing and the situation was getting tight and uncomfortable, Mr Kovacs went to the police and asked for an emigrant's passport – in itself rather a daring step. No one ventured to admit, of course, that he wanted to leave the country because life was easier and better abroad.

'And where do you want to emigrate to, Mr Kovacs?' the police superintendent asked him.

'To Holland.'

'Aren't you happy here?'

'Well, I can't complain.'

'Don't you have a good job?'

'I can't complain.'

'Don't you have a pleasant life?'

'I can't complain.'

'Then why do you want to emigrate to Holland?'

'Because there I *can* complain.'

The situation went from bad to worse, the terror of the secret police – the notorious AVO – became intolerable – the knock on the door became more and more frequent, people were arrested left and right for crimes they had never committed but to which under brutal torture they all confessed.

It became known that a mysterious three-fold coffin had been found at the bottom of the Danube. It had been long thought that Attila the Hun – a revered hero in Hungary – was buried there and it had always been hoped that one day his triple coffin might be found.

'The man in the coffin,' people told one another, 'is definitely Attila the Hun.'

'How can you be so sure?'

'He confessed.'

At one stage during the Hungarian uprising, the Russians declared that they would withdraw and indeed started to do so. Then they changed their minds, turned back and on 4 November 1956, reappeared in Budapest with armoured units, tanks, machine guns and field-guns, causing havoc, fire and death. But their propaganda kept on repeating: 'We are coming as friends.'

The wry Budapest comment was:

'That's lucky. Imagine how they would behave if they were coming as enemies.'

Twelve years later the Russians invaded the country of even better friends of theirs, the Czechoslovaks. Their excuse was even flimsier – all the lying pretexts collapsed and they failed to find the Quislings needed on such occasions.

'Do you know why the Russian army invaded Czechoslovakia?' people asked.

'Why?'

'To find the Czech who called them in.'

It is easy to see that these jokes are a highly effective manifestation of the critical spirit; in addition to giving vent to this spirit they help to maintain it. As long as a society can react to aggression, oppression and horror with this healthy spirit of scepticism, mockery and cynicism, its spirit is far from broken. The jokes may be a shade less lively than they used to be, and now and then they may become repetitive; but as long as the quality of the spirit remains excellent, never mind the quality of the jokes.

The Prince Primate

I feel another word – in fact, essentially a postscript to the foregoing
chapter – would not be out of place.

Budapest gained its reputation during two heroic periods: the first
lasted from the turn of the century to the middle of the First World
War and the second occurred during the nineteen thirties. It was not
only jokes but a peculiar, happy-go-lucky atmosphere, a refusal to face
realities in a collapsing world-order and a perhaps unjustified, but
completely natural, gaiety. There may have been a 'let's have a good
time while we can' desperation behind it all, but no desperation was
noticeable.

Lajos Zilahy, the brilliant playwright and novelist whose saga, *The
Dukays*, was a great success in the West, is an inexhaustible supply of
Budapest stories. He says that as soon as he has time to write a hundred
volumes he will compile a collection of these anecdotes; but less than
a hundred volumes will not do.

My favourite story from those heroic and mock-heroic times concerns
Gyula Krudy, a Hungarian Proust, the hero of many fantastic stories
and a bit of a legend by now. He was a huge man, well over six feet
tall, with a kind heart and an uncontrollable temper. He played cards
every night in the journalists' club and invariably lost all his money to
the very last penny. Borrowing was out of the question (he had already borrowed whatever he could, staked it on cards and lost it), so
night after night he had to go back on foot to his hotel room in the
Margaret Island. He just did not have the equivalent of twopence or
threepence for the tram. In the cruel, continental winter this was no
pleasant exercise. A colleague of his once asked him:

'And tell me, Gyula, when you walk there alone in the bitter cold, in

the snow, at three or four in the morning, without a single penny in your pocket, aren't you afraid?'
'Afraid of what?'
'Aren't you afraid that you might rob someone?'

A number of stories concern Janos Czernoch. In the days when these stories began, Czernoch was a small priest from Northern Hungary, today in Slovakia, and a Slovak peasant himself. For one reason or another he became friendly with a number of journalists and he, too, went to play cards regularly at the journalists' club, called Otthon ('Home'). One evening Czernoch – a poor, provincial priest – lost 10,000 crowns to a journalist and declared that he could not pay.
'What do you mean, you cannot pay?' he was asked. 'You come here to play cards, you take your winnings – if any – but when you lose you sit there and say you cannot pay?'
Czernoch was adamant, he said the 10,000 crowns was too much for him, he could not possibly pay even if he wanted to. The argument went on and Czernoch in the end declared:
'All right, I shall pay you the ten thousand if and when I become Prince Primate of Hungary.'
The Prince Primate of Hungary was the highest ecclesiastical dignitary of the land. A proper prince who had precedence over the Prime Minister – and he was also a very rich man. Czernoch, of course, felt pretty safe when he made this promise: he knew he had not the slightest chance even of being invited to Esztergom to *speak* to the Prince Primate. But a few years passed and Czernoch became a bishop; then an archbishop, and eventually the Slovak priest *was* elevated to the highest rank and became Prince Primate of Esztergom. The inauguration of a new Prince Primate was always a tremendous event during the days of the Monarchy but this time the press felt particularly jubilant: wasn't it, after all, their old pal and boon-companion who had reached these dazzling heights?
The Basilica of Esztergom was full for the inaugural Mass, with royalty, nobility, the judiciary and other great dignitaries of the land, but the first rows on the sides were reserved for journalists. Among them sat the man to whom Czernoch owed the ten thousand. At the most solemn moment of the Mass, the new Prince Primate – in his scarlet and gold robe – turned towards the congregation and raised his two arms aloft in blessing. His eyes fell on the journalist who, in turn,

raised *his* hands with his ten fingers displayed unmistakably reminding the new Prince of the Church of his debt. Czernoch raised his arms high and, looking the journalist firmly in the eye, shook his hands firmly, as if saying: *No, even now I am not going to pay.* Then he turned back to the High Altar and went on with the inaugural Mass, in the presence of His Majesty Francis Joseph I.

A reception followed to which the journalist was also invited. Czernoch did not talk to him but kept watching him from the corner of his eye. Finally, the journalist said good-bye to Czernoch who unexpectedly embraced him with touching warmth and vehemence. Everybody was amazed at this display of deep affection. Another embrace followed and then yet another.

The reason for this show of affection was that the journalist, wishing to compensate himself – however wrongly – for his loss, had filled his pockets with the Prince Primate's excellent Havana cigars, culled from the heavy silver boxes set all over the palace. Czernoch had noticed this and now, with his warm and triple embrace, had ensured that all the cigars in the man's pockets were crushed flat.

These, if perhaps not the best jokes, are surely the most characteristic. Where this impish verve permeates even the Prince Primate, there is a very special spirit in the air. No one can imagine an Archbishop of Canterbury behaving in the same way and Czernoch, in spite of these stories, was a truly great dignitary of the Church and a memorable Prince Primate. All these stories, whether they concerned Prince Primates or journalists or actors or other characters, were the same: ebullient, funny, reckless and always contained a slightly disreputable element, such as failure to pay one's debts, seducing other men's wives, stealing cigars – and a million other variations.

This was the spirit from which the reputation of the Budapest joke grew. This spirit may grow occasionally tired but it survives and still has, every now and then, its moments of glory.

The respectable middle class may shake their heads and view all this with doubt and misgiving. Yet, a country and an era where the Prince Primate, at the most solemn moment of his life, is able to inform a journalist friend that he does not intend to settle a gambling debt, has certainly earned a place for itself in the history of humour. This tradition deserves not only our amusement, our smiles, our 'sociological' interest, but also our . . . well, I nearly said respect. . . . But as its main glory is that it teaches us not to respect anything; not to take anything too seriously – how can it deserve our respect? If it teaches us anything, it teaches that even the most solemn moment of the High Mass has its humour and if God exists at all, He must be a humorous old boy who – at that moment – must have looked perhaps not entirely without amazement but surely with a twinkle in His eyes at His new Prince Primate. That era and that tradition deserve our warm, affectionate and tender non-respect.

The repartee

There are three types of jokes – and humour – I should like to say something about.

The first is the sick joke. I admit, I do not like it. I am surprised at myself because there is nothing in sick jokes which goes against the grain in me, which is against my theories as laid down here; but there is usually something that goes against my taste. I do not hold that there are subjects which must not be joked about: on the contrary, I have tried to explain that as I see it, every subject under the sun – including illness, religion and death – is a legitimate subject for a joke. When I talk of 'taste', I do not have prudish Victorian taste in mind. Jokes may shock and indeed if they want to keep their reputation as one of the minor arts, they must shock. The word 'catharsis' cannot possibly apply to jokes; but they can produce minor shocks, cause sudden insights which improve our vision of the world; they can reveal and they can illuminate. They cannot slaughter sacred cows but they can irritate and wound them, occasionally drive them mad and hurt them deeply.

What is my quarrel with sick jokes? Simply that they are too self-conscious. They are the jokes of the eternal show-offs who tell these jokes winking at us as if they were saying: 'Look at us, how brave, how progressive, how unconventional we are! We make fun of things most people hardly dare mention.' It is not only that I suspect a great deal of cowardice underlies these 'brave' jokes but there is something of the sixth form in them. I am quite prepared to judge them as jokes, as humour and as such they may be bad or good; but they are not content to be judged on that basis: they think that their very sickness secures them some superiority over ordinary humour and anyone who fails to laugh at rotting corpses, cancer and necrophilia, is a hopeless petit-bourgeois and square. But a man who cannot think of anything funnier when he is in the mood for humour than rotting corpses or cancer and tries to turn *that* into a joke is not a born humorist but a born bore. I saw one of these sick comedies in which corpses were dragged across the stage and the death of young people was regarded as a great giggle. Before going I had wondered whether I would take to it kindly or would be repelled. In the event, I was simply bored stiff. It was a bad play.

You can laugh even at death and cancer in certain circumstances; but death and cancer are not funny *per se*. And anybody who thinks they are is not a man with an exquisite sense of humour but a neurotic trying to be funny.

The second type of humour I want to mention briefly is nonsense. A nonsense joke may be mild and sweet, perhaps not even too nonsensical. To the horror of the proprietor and the waiters, a man at one of the restaurant tables starts putting the spinach on his head. The proprietor goes up to him and asks him, politely but firmly, what he thinks he is doing.

'What do you mean, what I am doing?'

'Well, sir, why are you putting the spinach on your head?'

'Good gracious, is this spinach? I thought it was apple pie.'

From this, one can graduate to the glorious and immortal nonsense of Edward Lear. Take the *Akond of Swat* or *The Owl and the Pussy-cat* or almost any verse from vintage Lear, like this verse 5 from *The Jumblies*:

> They sailed to the Western Sea, they did,
>   To a land all covered with trees,
> And they bought an Owl, and a useful Cart,
> And a pound of Rice, and a Cranberry Tart,
>   And a hive of silvery Bees.
> And they bought a Pig, and some green Jack-daws,
> And a lovely Monkey with lollipop paws,
> And forty bottles of Ring-Bo-Ree,
> And no end of Stilton Cheese.
> Far and few, far and few,
> Are the land where the Jumblies live;

> Their heads are green, and their hands are blue,
> And they went to sea in a Sieve.

Lear was a true poet whom some put into the Wordsworth class. Just here we are concerned with his nonsense only. Nonsense has been analysed many times. A short while ago I was asked to write a kind of documentary script on humour for BBC Television. The powers that be liked my script (and paid for it) but never used it. In that script Edward Lear was to have appeared in person to explain his own theory of nonsense. I think the best I can do is to quote the words of Edward Lear himself – words he never spoke:

'I am very grateful for this chance' (as Lear never said). 'As I died in 1888, I had no previous chance of explaining this on television. Nor did I myself know all I know today. Nonsensification is, of course, an escape from reality. My own personal reality – from which I meant to escape – was loneliness. I always professed to love and prefer loneliness but – looking back – I believe I only feared people. The other stark reality I had to escape was impecuniousness. We might as well call it poverty. But whatever the motives of escape, nonsense makes only sense if it creates a higher reality; today people might call it surreality. (Or was it yesterday they called it that?)

'I think I may claim that my own nonsense world has its own reality, with its own laws. It is a proper, well-ordered world. There is no nonsense about my nonsense. It is a world that does not exist; will never exist; cannot exist. But it is a world which ought to exist.'

My own ideal and favourite – and third subject – is the repartee. Repartee is a witty and smart reply, a lightning retort.

Now let us all admit that the *ésprit d'escalier* is much more frequent a phenomenon than the true repartee. We usually think of the right answer on the staircase and we are doubly furious for not having thought of it before.

On this terrain the writer enjoys an advantage over everyone else. *He* thinks of the brilliant and devastating answer a week later and yet, he can recount the scene as if he had given the answer immediately. You can never beat a writer, not at least according to the testimony of his own writings. He is always witty; always brilliant; he always wins. In 1936 I was deeply offended by a man in Budapest. His remark really wounded me and it rankled. I kept thinking of that scene of humiliation and could never get over it. Then, suddenly, in 1966, I thought of a brilliant riposte. I was thirty years late, but repartee is repartee. I wrote a little sketch in which I was insulted, but my devastating answer – which came to me in a flash nearly three decades later – was, of course, prompt and off the cuff. It's amazing how much wittier you become if you have thirty years to work out an answer. But I got it all out of my system. As far as I am concerned, I won that encounter.

About Parliamentary repartee, I am always a little sceptical. I have a vague feeling that it is never as prompt as it seems. When Sheridan said to Henry Dundas:

'The Right Honourable Gentleman is indebted to his memory for his jests and to his imagination for his facts' – he was being certainly witty enough but Sheridan had all the time in the world to think that one out. Who imagines – indeed, who is prepared to believe – that he thought of it on the spur of the moment?

Harold Macmillan describes in his *Memoirs* that during Churchill's second Premiership, he walked once into the Cabinet room and found the Prime Minister absorbed in work. Churchill explained: 'I am working on my impromptues for this afternoon.' And he added: 'Hard work.'

Winston Churchill had seen the tiny Sidney Silverman – whose legs did not reach the floor when he was sitting on his seat in the House – jump off, or jump up many times. Interrupted one day by Silverman, Churchill shouted at him: 'The Hon. Member should not be so ready to hop down off his perch!'

Another famous Parliamentary remark – I do not remember who said it to whom but it has been quoted many times – does not sound impromptu either: 'The Right Honourable Gentleman has sat for so long on the fence that the iron has entered his soul.'

For a Parliamentary retort that sounds quite genuinely quick, let us quote the aristocratic member who shouted (quite a few years ago) to an Irish Member: 'The Hon. Member will die either of venereal disease or on the gallows.' To which the man replied:

'That depends on whether I embrace the Hon. Member's mistress or his principles.'

F. E. Smith gave many wonderfully quick answers to judges – a brave thing for a young barrister to do – but these have been quoted over and over again.

One of Churchill's Parliamentary repartees is almost as well known but I cannot resist quoting it (from memory). Lady Astor shouted at him after an acrimonious exchange:

'If the Right Honourable Gentleman were my husband, I'd put arsenic in his coffee.'

To which Churchill replied:

'If the Honourable Lady were my wife, I'd drink it.'

The repartee can, occasionally, be not only witty but also wise. Take the well-known rejoinder between the society lady and the drunk gentleman:

Man: 'You are revoltingly ugly, Madam.'

Woman: 'And you are disgustingly drunk.'

Man: 'But I shall be sober tomorrow.'

A plea for humour

All things considered, it is a pity that humour is dead. If it is still possible, it would be worth rescuing it.

I have two chief reasons for my plea.

The pleasant and praiseworthy elements of humour – a sense of proportion, an ability to laugh at yourself and to see yourself as others see you – speak for themselves. But the more offensive elements also have their bright side.

It is true that laughter nearly always has a malicious element in it. When someone in the Bible said that he who laughs last, laughs longest, he had this malicious type of laughter in mind and knew what he was talking about. Laughter can be aggressive and indeed I am inclined to go as far as to say that it cannot be anything else.

This, however, is a further reason for cherishing it and keeping it alive.

Some of us must have noticed that human nature is not altogether peerless and angelic. It simply needs to get rid of a certain amount of nastiness and malice: so why not laugh it off?

We have heard a great deal about the brutalizing effect of certain television shows and comics. They indeed can be brutalizing and I am sure that some of these films and strips have given ideas to young people how to rob, steal, cheat and kill. But on the whole – if they are produced with just a little intelligence and restraint, they have quite a different effect. Love of adventure and fantasy is gratified by Westerns and by the crimes, murders or brave and noble deeds committed vicariously.

Similarly, there is nothing really wrong with aggressiveness. As I said before: our forest-dweller ancestors would not have survived without it and still less our city-dweller contemporaries. And whether it is good or bad, it is part of human nature. We *are* all aggressive – however angelic and guileless we like to imagine ourselves. Some, of course, are worse than others. Some people become highway- or bank-robbers to gratify their aggressive impulse; others beat up their girl friends with whips; others become dictators and start world wars; and others again make jokes.

Jokes are better than wars. Even the most aggressive jokes are better than the least aggressive wars. Even the longest jokes are better than the shortest wars.

Now, more than a quarter of a century after the last war, we only remember the exciting highlights and forget that one of war's worst aspects is that it is so terribly boring. Even the liveliest wars are more boring than the dullest jokes.

But my plea for humour is not only a negative one. Humanity loves laughing. Wise men (including myself) have explained that they are mistaken. Laughter is a silly reflex. It is useless. Painful. Nasty. Exhausting. Primitive. It is better to smile. It is better to weep. It is better to sob and have a jolly good catharsis.

It is all true, all wise, all brilliantly thoughtful. But humanity still wants to laugh.

We want people to laugh *with us* because we know that you love the man who makes you laugh. And we all want love – that's what this whole big show – called the world and life – is about.

The smile may be superior; it may be more intellectual; worthier of the serious humorist who, after all, is 'just another writer'. But whatever we say – indeed, whatever we believe – it is your laughter we are after, because you always put your heart in your laughter and we want your heart.

Humour, I think, is responsible for more important human advance than physics, medicine or any other science. It teaches us to see things in proportion. Do not despise anyone: the great and the small, the powerful and the humble, the rich and poor – the millionaire and the *schnorrer* of the Jewish jokes – are all the same people really: all are likeable because all are funny. But no one is truly awe-inspiring; no one is really *that* impressive; authority should be fooled, fought against and not revered.

I finish with the joke of jokes. It is not the best of all jokes but in a sense the most important.

A Jew goes to the Rabbi in despair and tells him that his son wants to get baptized – regarded as the worst of all blows.

'Well,' says the Rabbi, 'look at my own son.'

'What do you mean?' asks the Jew astonished. 'You do not mean that your own son, Rabbi, wants to get baptized?'

'Yes, that is exactly what I do mean.'

'And what did you do when you heard this?'

'What can a Rabbi do? I turned to God.'

'And what did God tell you?'

'Exactly what I have told you: look at my own son.'

This joke cuts God down to size. He, too, is troubled by the new generation; He, too, is worried. This joke rebels against authority but – in the true manner of jokes – rebels with charm and wit: hits at authority yet makes authority more, not less, likeable.

The non-humorous world has one ambition. Every humourless member of it wants to be godlike; nay: wants to be God. Humour, at its best, teaches us that this is not a worth-while ambition: God himself is only human.

And that's where Humour becomes Divine. Perhaps our belief in that human God humour gives us – a God who is just as worried about Jesus, i.e. the next generation, as we are about our children – is less fervent; but we like Him more.

References

1 For a detailed study of these theories see J. Y. T. Greig, *The Psychology of Laughter and Comedy*, London 1923.

2 Dr Martin Grotjahn, *Beyond Laughter*, New York 1966.

3 Oscar Wilde, *Selected Works*, edited by Richard Aldington, London 1946.

4 R. M. and A. W. Yerkes, *The Great Apes*, New Haven 1929.

5 Arthur Koestler, *The Act of Creation*, London 1964.

6 Dr Martin Grotjahn, 'Jewish Jokes and their Relation to Masochism', *Journal of the Hillside Hospital*, New York 1961.

7 Theodor Reik, *Jewish Wit*, New York 1962.